All Israel Dances Toward the Tabernacle

by

Chester Anderson and Tina Clemens

ALL ISRAEL DANCES TOWARD THE TABERNACLE
by Chester Anderson and Tina Clemens
© 2001, Simchat Adonai Dance Ministry, Belleview, FL.

Published by:
Key of David Publishing, Saint Cloud, FL
Printed in the United States of America.
Distributed by:
Key of David, PO Box 700217, Saint Cloud, FL, 34770
Phone: 1.800.829.8777   http://www.mim.net

Simchat Adonai Dance Ministry and

Tina Clemens
www.GroomedforRoyalty.org
352.746.5328
tina@groomedforroyalty.org

Ministries:

Chester Anderson
joybubbles@cheerful.com   Tina Clemens

Cover design by Crystal Lenhart.   Interior illustrations by Amanda Lundy, © 2001 by Simchat Adonai Dance Ministries. All rights reserved.

ISBN 1-886987-09-2

"I will build
you up again and
you will be rebuilt,
O Virgin Israel.
Again you will take
up your tambourines
and go out to dance
with the joyful"
(Jeremiah 31:4, NIV).

Dedication

The finished product you hold in your hands,
I believe to be nothing less than a miracle.
One chapter at a time, they seemed to just pop out of me or
my co-author. Then we would send portions back and forth
to each other. We would be as thrilled as little kids, as we
read with delight each of the new section.

Having read the finished manuscript, we are in awe!
Who wrote this book? Surely the One Who penned it is the
Holy Spirit. Really, His name should be on the cover, not
ours. And so to His credit we bow and give honor!
Forever!

We dedicate this work to our Heavenly Father,
Yahweh our King!
We will reign with Him forever!
We love you Father!!

Contents

Preface

Driving down the road after work one Sunday night I heard a voice. It was a very familiar voice. The voice that I heard was mine, and I heard myself say, "You are going to write a book." Totally excited I drove home and approached my mother and began talking to her. I started by asking a question, "Mother, can you guess what I am going to do?" As she looked up, she said, "You are going to write a book." Amazed, I asked, "How did you know?" "The Father told me" she replied.

Around this same time Simchat Adonai Dance Ministries was in the midst of preparations for a dance workshop. I instructed my leaders to prepare a lesson on what the Father would give them for the workshop. One leader, Tina Clemens, was about to begin one of the most exciting adventures in her life.

The more she listened to the Father and stayed pure in His sight, the more He reveled to her. As the dance workshop got closer, she was the first to send me her notes for the workshop she would be teaching, called, "Spiritual Warfare in Dance," or "The Dancing Warrior."

Her lesson was all typed out on several pages with a title and subtitles on each page. When I first read it, it was a hurried reading, and I must say that I did not even grasp the concept about which she was writing.

The Day of the Dance Workshop Arrived:

Gathering my lessons from various note books I began to speak. I spoke on entering into the presence of Yahweh, who we put value in, and Miriam, Moses' sister. I talked about why we dance, where dance is mentioned in Scripture, and why we should look to Miriam as a role model and leader. Afterward, we went into the other building and danced.

Tina was next to speak before lunch. I still remember the excitement in her voice as she spoke from the bema (platform). With great enthusiasm she spoke on the *Dancing Warrior*. I was in awe as I listened. Never had I heard the exciting words that were coming from her mouth. She captivated the audience. When it was time to leave they begged for more. Could this be the same Tina that I have been dancing with for three years?

She was a new Tina. A new joy had entered her life.

By the end of the workshop, I knew that I was going to write my book on what God told me. I was going to write on Dance. Simple, right?

At the time I thought it would be.

The next week, I came to practice, all excited about the new project that I wanted to work on and I told the other dancers. Also, I Tina that I wanted her to work on the project with me. She looked at me and said, "*Hummmm...*

From that time forward, the Father gave Tina and I chapter after chapter. He gave us what He wanted to be in "His dance book."

As we turned our notes from the workshop into chapters, we saw how the Father was cultivating us, how He was bringing us to a new level of understanding in Him. It is a level that can only be reached by studying and meditating on His Word. We get there only by striving to enter into the Holy of Holies.

Never in my dreams did I ever imagine that the Father would use me. Me, a kid from Ocala, Florida, one who still lives with his parents. He has allowed me to seek out His truths, ones that have been hidden for ages.

In your hands is what I believe to be a "masterpiece." I say this not because we did it, but because I truly believe the Father has granted us, His vessels, the opportunity to write down His truths about dance.

As you read, we pray you will be blessed and encouraged; we pray you will seek out the new but old truths about praise and worship through dance. This book is just a glimpse of what is to come, till in His Day "All Israel Dances Toward The Tabernacle."

Chester Anderson
Belleview, FL

All Israel Dances Toward The Tabernacle

Introduction

To help you understand the perspective from which this book was written, we will touch on a few topics:

The Name Game

Before writing this book, we took into account the considerable amount of research available on the accurate name of our Heavenly Father. We read books, listened to tapes, and studied. We found that some show proof the Name is YHVH, spelled out as Yahveh, or Yahovah. Others have piles of evidence that the correct Name is YHWH, spelled out as Yahweh, while some just shorten it to "Yah." Some use ADONAI, LORD, HaShem, El and God (which are titles and not proper names). The challenge continues with the proper spelling and sound of His Son's Name. Songs are sung about Yeshua, Yahshua, Y'shua, and Jesus. And this is only a partial listing of the Names used for the Father and the Son!

In this work we use many of the above names. This is not to bring confusion, but to make a peaceful appeal to our wide range of readers. The point is, when each one of us turned our will over to the Savior and 'got saved,' we called on a Name. Did He hear us?

Our book deals with dance and it's place in the lives of Believers who have trusting faith in and live for the Great I AM, the LORD God of Avraham/Abraham, Yitz'chak/Isaac and Ya'akov/Jacob. Therefore, this study material will not address which name is correct, nor try to prove which name you should choose. It is each Believer's responsibility to make that decision. Yeshua/Yahshua/ Jesus called His heavenly Father "Abba" (Mark 14:36; Romans 8:14-15; Galatians 4:6). We suggest everyone become familiar this "Daddy" title. We hope everyone will come to personally know Him as their "Abba," their Father.

What name do we personally use? Do you call your biological father by his first name? Most call their father, Dad, Daddy or Father. They do not call Him Harry or Joe. The name 'Abba' is an endearment used only by one's children, not by slaves. (*See Dake's Annotated Reference Bible* at each scripture location). 'Abba' is a personal and intimate name. It is one we like to use.

Translations

We have found, as you probably have found, errors in study references and Bible translations. But rather than focus on the flaws, let's be grateful we have so many resources available to us! "From everyone who has been given much, much will be demanded; and from the one who has been entrusted with much, much more will be asked" (Luke 12:48, NIV).

As to Scriptures, most often we use the New International Version (NIV) (we have the software on that one), and the Complete Jewish Bible (CJB).

The Hebrew Language

Precious treasures are the rewards of diligent and persistent studying. We are no longer satisfied with merely the surface meaning of Abba's Word. Are you? This increased hunger comes from Him.   Now that we understand the plain and simple (foundational) meaning, let us go on to the deeper things of Yah (Hebrews 6:1-3). One aspect of digging deeper is getting to the root meaning of Hebrew words. *Strong's Concordance* is a reliable study companion that anyone can easily use, and which we use repeatedly in this book. We hope you will acquire a hunger to reach into the rich Hebrew meanings of the Holy Scriptures.   David Stern's translation of the *Complete Jewish Bible* is helpful for Hebrew names, which reveal a deeper meaning beyond the English translations.

We find that, often while studying the Holy Spirit takes us on adventure trails that seem to end in an empty field.   Then, later (sometimes years later) He takes us back there, only to find buried treasure. Many times, we can't even remember how we arrived at that conclusion. All this makes studying FUN.

In order to boost knowledge of Hebrew names and terminology we will insert the English name after the Hebrew for the first time it is used in each chapter. The remainder of the usage in that chapter will be Hebrew. For example Ya'akov is the Hebrew name for Jacob. You will find his name printed as Ya'akov/Jacob the first time we refer to him in any given chapter. *Ruach HaKodesh* is the Hebrew for Holy Spirit. Sometimes we refer to Him simply as Ruach, Spirit.

The Two Houses of Israel
Ephraim and Judah

While preparing for a dance workshop Abba kept bringing the words" Israel" and "dance" to me. As I prayed He opened my eyes and mind to see Israel in the dance. Since that time I have come to understand that, before we can truly comprehend dance as worship to the Father, we need to understand Israel in all its fulness, because they are His "chosen people." They are called to dance before Him in all their unified glory.

If this is the first time you have heard about "both the houses of Israel" (Isaiah 8:14), this may sound awkward at first, but by the end of our journey it will be clear to you. To understand Israel we will start with Father Avraham/Abraham.

From Exalted Father to Father of Many

"Your name shall no longer be called Abram, but your name shall be Abraham, for I have made you the father of many nations" (Genesis 17:5, TSET).

We see that Yah has called Avraham to be the father of many nations—a father whose children would one day fill the world and have his same love for God.

The name, Avram/Abram represents his former status as a "high and exalted father. "

Avraham represents his new status as the "father of a multitude."

In the New Covenant/New Testament Paul speaks of Avraham being a Father to a multitude of peoples (Romans 4:12-22).

Ya'akov/ Israel

Avraham would be the Father of a multitude of nations. His son Yitz'chak/Isaac was blessed with the same promise of multiplicity of his seed (Genesis 26:24). From Yitz'chak seed we will see Abba's promise to Avraham being fulfilled, through Ya'akov/Jacob. Ya'akov will lead us to the name "Israel." Ya'akov had twelve sons, and from his sons came the twelve tribes of Israel. All of Ya'akov's ancestors received their name from the founding father of the tribe from which they were born. This is what is called an eponymic (example: Levi is one of the sons of Ya'akov. Levi's ancestors are called the Levites). Yah changed Ya'akov's name to Israel; therefore his sons became the children of "Israel" meaning that their father is Ya'akov/Israel. Just as Avraham received a promise from Yah that nations would descend from him, Ya'akov/Israel received the same promise (Genesis 35:11).

Is Judah All Israel?

Israel was not all Jewish; there is no scripture reference in the Bible that refers to all Israel being Jewish. All Jews are Israelites but not all Israelites are Jews. It is very important to grasp this concept in order to understand what the Father has planned for His people. The first "Jew" in the Bible was Y'hudah/Judah (Genesis 29:35). Y'hudah was one of the twelve sons of Ya'akov-Israel. Y'hudah's descendants, or the tribe of Judah, are the Jews.

Example: Y'hudah had a brother by the name of Naftali/ Naphtali. Naftali's children were known as the Naftalites. Naftali's children and Y'hudah's children would be cousins to each other. The same is true for Joseph and Judah. The point is, tribal affiliation did not change, ever. However, once Yahveh divided Israel into two houses, the twelve tribes were thereafter collectively known as Israel (Joseph/ Ephraim) and/or Judah. Yah chose Israel to be His chosen people. All twelve tribes make up those chosen people, and Israel was divided into two "houses."

Who, Then, is Israel? — A Family Feud

A brief explanation needs to be given to clarify our stance on "Who is Israel."

Have you ever felt lost in your Bible when reading about the wars between the kings of the north and south? Has it been challenging to keep straight which king was 'good' and which king was 'bad'? The key to a clearer understanding lies in the book of 1 Kings chapter Eleven. Understanding this event is pivotal to understanding all of Yahweh's Word. Occurring approximately 921 BC, here we find a detailed explanation of how the prophet came to Jeroboam, tore his cloak into twelve pieces and foretold the future family split. (For an exciting study about the two houses of Israel, Ephraim and Judah, see the compelling book, *Who Is Israel?* by Batya Wootten, 2000, Key of David, Saint Cloud, FL.)

The twelve pieces of the cloak represented the twelve tribes of Israel. In 922 BC, ten of those pieces, or tribes, led by Jeroboam, broke off from the United Kingdom of Israel. Jeroboam became the king of Northern Israel and set up religious centers at Beth El and Dan. King Rehoboam remained king of Judah where Jerusalem became the capital (1 Kings 12:1-33).

Following is a brief recap/description of these two nations:

A. The Northern House or Kingdom:

- Called Israel, or Ephraim because Ephraim was given the birthright (1 Chronicles 5:1-2; Ezekiel 37:19) and so had the "birthright" name, "Israel" (Genesis 48:19,22; Exodus 4:22; Jeremiah 31:18-19).
- Primarily consisted of ten of the tribes, or families, of Israel (1 Kings 11:31; Judges 12:5).
- Assimilated and intermingled with the nations. Adopted pagan practices.
- Abandoned Hebraic identity, the God of Israel, and Torah (God's instructions).
- Broke family ties with brothers.
- Scattered because of sin in 721 BC. Assimilated or "lost" among the Assyrians (2 Kings 17).
- Destined to become "Sons of the Living God" (Hosea 1-2).

B. The Southern House or Kingdom:

- Called Judah; primarily made up of two of the tribes, or families, of Israel; referred to as "Jews" (1 Kings 12:21).

- Stayed more faithful to Yahweh's Torah. Preserved the Holy Scripture.
- Retained Hebraic identity.
- Would not intermingle with pagan nations.

C. Both the Northern and the Southern houses have sinned:

- Yahweh rejected both houses of Israel (Jeremiah 3:17-18, 11:16-17). "The two families that HASHEM had chosen, He has rejected them" (Jeremiah 33:24, TSET).

D. The Two Houses of Israel are Yahweh's "Witnesses" and He has an exciting latter-day plan for the two of them:

- "'You are My witnesses,' declares the LORD, 'And My servant whom I have chosen, So that you may know and believe Me And understand that I am He. Before Me there was no God formed, and there will be none after Me" (Isaiah 43:10,12; 44:8, NASB).
- Scripture calls for "two" or more witnesses for a matter to be confirmed in the earth: Moses said, "A single witness shall not rise up against a man...on the evidence of two or three witnesses a matter shall be confirmed. Yeshua said, "It is written that the testimony of two persons is reliable and valid." And Shual/Paul said, "Every matter must be established by the testimony of two or three witnesses" (Deuteronomy 19:15; John 8:17; 2 Corinthians 13:1, NASB).
- Israel was divided into two families, nations, houses (Jeremiah 33:24; Ezekiel 37:22; Isaiah 8:13-14).
- The Father has sworn that He will make the "two sticks" that represent both the houses of Israel, Ephraim and Judah, "one stick in His hand" (Ezekiel 37:15-28).

The problem has been that the "family feud" that has existed between the two houses of Israel has continued up until this day. However, we are blessed to live in the generation that is beginning to see the restoration of that family! That family is ISRAEL! Ezekiel forecasts that restoration in his 37th chapter, when Yahweh declared that He will take the two sticks and make them one in His hand. On these two sticks He writes the names of the two families, Ephraim on one stick and Judah on the other stick.

The feud has been over who is ISRAEL? The plain and simple truth is that both houses/kingdoms are ISRAEL. This is why we are dancing! This is why all the celebration is happening! ALL ISRAEL is being restored to all the promises our Father has for us!

In Acts Fifteen we find Amos 9:11 quoted; which speaks of the restoration of David's tabernacle. When a dispute arose among the Early Believers about "Gentiles" being brought into Israel's Renewed Covenant community, Kefa/Peter and Ya'acov/James addressed the Body, and Ya'akov said, "Simon has described to us how God at first showed his concern by taking from the Gentiles a people for himself. The words of the prophets are in agreement with this, as it is written: 'After this I will return and rebuild David's fallen tent. Its ruins I will rebuild, and I will restore it, that the remnant of men may seek the Lord, and all the Gentiles who bear my name, says the Lord, who does these things'" (Acts 15:14-18, NIV).

The Father looks upon each of His children equally. He chose Israel to be His children. Take a moment to imagine what it would be like if Judah had been like Ephraim. If Judah had been bound by paganism and assimilated into the nations of the world, would we still have our Torah? What would life be like without our Old/First Covenant Scriptures? For this reason we are grateful to Judah and we stand by our Jewish brothers. Judah returned to Yah after her Babylonian exile. Judah preserved Torah so that the world might have a relationship with the Heavenly Father.

On the other hand, let us imagine if Ephraim had been like Judah and had not accepted Jesus as Messiah. The world at large would not have heard of the only begotten Son (of the Creator) if not for Ephraim's efforts.

As prophesied, both houses have "stumbled over the "Sanctuary" (Isaiah 8:14). And yet both have been used by the Almighty. Both have good to contribute to the whole that will be a fully restored Israel.

Brothers! Let us learn to walk hand and hand, united as ONE!

To The Tabernacle

Where are We Headed? Some would say the Ark of the Covenant is the heart of the world. Have you heard this? If you believe Yahshua/Jesus is the Messiah of Israel then you are on the way to the Holy of Holies or Most Holy Place.

"'After this I will return and rebuild David's fallen tent. Its ruins I will rebuild, and I will restore it, that the remnant of men may seek the Lord, and all the Gentiles who bear my name, says the Lord, who does these things' that have been known for ages" (Acts 15:16-18, NIV).

Here the apostle Ya'akov/James is quoting from the prophet Amos 9:11-12. The word used by the NIV translators is 'tent' whereas KJV uses the word 'tabernacle.' The Greek word used for tabernacle in the 'refreshed' or New Testament is *Strong's* word #G4633 meaning a tent or cloth hut (literal. or figuratively): - habitation, tabernacle. Comes from #G4632 and #G4639.

#G4632 meaning a vessel, implement, equipment or apparatus (literal or figuratively [spec. a wife as contributing to the usefulness of the husband]); -goods, sail, stuff, vessel.

#G4639 meaning "shade" or a shadow (literal or figuratively [darkness or error or an adumbration]): - shadow.

We have discovered, largely Hebrew authors, with an understanding of Hebrew expressions, composed our New Covenant/New Testament, which was written in Greek. In order to make sense of some phrases, we will need to reach through the Greek to the underlying Hebrew expressions. So let's see what we discover from the Old Testament passage in Amos about the Hebrew definition for the word 'tabernacle.' *Strong's* tells us #H5521 is sukkah meaning a hut or lair: - booth, cottage, cover, pavilion, tabernacle, tent. It is the feminine of #H5520 rooted in #H5526 meaning a proposition. to entwine as a screen; by implication to fence in, cover over, (figuratively) protect: - cover, defense, defend, hedge in, join together, set, shut up. The restoration of David's fallen tent is in progress. The restoration started on the day when Ya'akov quotes Amos 9:11 in Acts 15.

Are you excited to be smack in the middle of fulfilled prophecy? We are headed to the sukkah (of love), or chuppah ('hoo-paw'), the marriage canopy of Yahshua, our Heavenly Bridegroom!

Preparation

God's Word speaks to us in allegories, metaphors, word pictures, parables, and dark sayings (Psalms 49:4; 78:2). "Let the wise listen and add to their learning, and let the discerning get guidance — for understanding proverbs and parables, the sayings and riddles of the wise" (Proverbs 1:5-6, NIV). The sanctuary we see pictured for us in the Old Testament is a shadow of the true sanctuary in heaven (Hebrews 8:5). The book of Hebrews would be worthwhile for us to study to help us get a tighter grasp on the things of the Older Testament. Our Father is simple enough for a child to understand. At the same time, He is intricate beyond our ability to grasp His complexity. Let us attempt to dig deeper into His holy ways though they be higher than ours are (Psalms 77:13; Isaiah 55:8).

The story of Queen Esther demonstrates to us, the Bride of Messiah, the proper manner to come into the King's presence. She is the type and shadow from the older to the newer illustration of the Bride. Look at the preparation she underwent prior to her presenting herself to the king for his approval (Ester 2:12-17). Later, when the plight was of a life and death situation, she boldly approached the king in the inner courtyard of his palace. She put on her royal robes coming to him on the third day (catch the significance here). We can see the reception she received from her king as it is recorded, "she won his favor" (Ester 5:1-3).

Both our hearts and our bodies must be prepared to step into the presence of our King. Considerable time is needed and serious value is placed on the preparedness of the Queen/Bride. Let us not forget this preparation as we study.

Waymaker

We are thrilled to stand on this side of Calvary. We delight in the lavish benefits obtained by our Heavenly Bridegroom. The way into the King's chambers has been provided by our Intercessor, our High Priest, Yahshua. He went into the Holy of Holies one time for us thus making the way possible for all who accept His finished work. There is a proper way to enter into the King's chambers today. We do not barge in with an arrogant and boastful approach. We do not come with an attitude as a cocky teenage wanting to get the keys to the family car. Many of us can remember the days when we were a demanding teenager who carried an 'attitude' toward our parents. Let us approach our King prepared, humble and confident He will accept us (1 John 3:21,22; Hebrews 10:22).

The Gold Room

The Tabernacle in the Wilderness contained three compart-ments (see Exodus starting in chapter twenty-seven for your personal study concerning the pattern of the earthy tabernacle).

These compartments were the outer court, the inner court and the Most Holy Place or Holy of Holies. Moshe/Moses was instructed, See that you make them according to the pattern shown you on the mountain" (Exodus 25:40, NIV). The chapters you are about to read progress from the outer court, to the inner court and finally into the Most Holy Place. It is natural for us, the worshiper, to desire to go deeper in our worship experience. We encourage you not to become complacent with an outer court experience in your worship. Our admonishment is the same as the writer in Hebrews 6:1 " … leaving behind the initial lessons about the Messiah, let us go on to maturity…." The priest of the Tabernacle in the Wilderness would fall down dead if he failed to complete his yearly duties correctly. After proper preparedness, we can enter into the gold room without fear of death. What a relief!

We are thrilled to present for your consideration the insight unveiled to us by the Father. We have been shown only a glimpse. Yet we eagerly wait the ongoing revealing of His end-time plan as the King completes the restoration of David's Tabernacle. Let ALL OF ISRAEL DANCE TOWARD THE TABERNACLE!

The Road Map

We are on a journey. If we do not know the route or our destination, we may very well end up somewhere else, or nowhere special. As both houses of Israel dance toward the Tabernacle of our God, YHVH, we are on the most momentous journey of our lives. This journey has been waiting to be completed for millennium.

Once we all arrive at the gates of the Tabernacle, our adventure is far from over. In fact, this last 'leg' of our pilgrimage is the most important of all. Using the pattern set forth by Moshe/Moses, we will continue this theme throughout our book. Of course, Moshe built YHVH's Tabernacle in the wilderness based on the pattern he was shown in heaven.

Make this tabernacle and all its furnishings exactly like the pattern I will show you (Exodus 25:9 NIV).

This is our King's pattern for worship. Though each one of us will proceed at different paces we must realize we are invited, one and all, into the King's private chambers. Once we are invited we have a choice to accept or decline. The gift of our free will enables us to be the kind of worshipers He is seeking. Is He calling you to press in?

The Outer Court

As soon as we see the Tabernacle from the distance, we are excited to rush up into it to see our Father. We have been praising Him with song and dance the entire trip and we just want to charge into His house. Ah! But wait. We find He has a prescribed fashion for us to enter.

Enter his gates with thanksgiving and his courts with praise; give thanks to him and praise his name (Psalms 100:4 NIV).

The Outer Court is a large open-aired courtyard full of excitement: loud praises, shouts of joy, tambourines, and song and dance. This court is packed with praisers. Our eyes drink in the beautiful array of streamers and flags of every color and size embellished with much fanfare and beauty. Our ears delight in the melody of instruments of all shapes and sounds. We quickly join the crowd with our own praises to our Father. What joy! What glory! We are so happy to meet our Heavenly Father here in His Outer Court. We are here at last!

After a while a few praisers begin to think, "Is this all there is? This is great! We love praising Abba here. But our spirits tell us there is MORE." Have you had this experienced while worshiping our King? This Outer Court worship experience is our first step to our goal; but it is not our goal. Let us press on past the praisers in the Outer Court into the next step of our worship experience.

The Inner Court

The first thing we notice in this new place of worship is the reduced size of this court. The Inner Court is so much smaller than the last place of worship. There are fewer worshipers here. The next observance we make is the air filled with fragrance; sweet, very sweet fragrance. The Inner Court is a room lit only by a seven-branched candlestick on one side. This candlestick amply lights the entire room, reflecting off the gold in-laid walls. It is a room of splendor! We conclude this room is very special. Even the worshipers are different in this room. We join them in their supplication, adoration and reverent worship of our Father and our King.

We feel we could stay here forever. We commune with our Father. We feast on His living bread, we bow down before Him to worship Him in all His glory. This is IT. But is it? After a long time, perhaps years, we notice there are a few worshipers gathering around the curtain dividing the Inner Court from the Holy of Holies. In front of this dividing curtain stands the altar from which we enjoy the aroma filling the room. The incense never ceases rising. But why is the altar placed right in the pathway of the entrance to the Holy of Holies? Why are a few worshipers gathering around this curtain? Could there be MORE to our worship experience?

The Holy of Holies

We press through the curtain. Have we reached our goal at last? The light is nearly blinding here in this magnificent place. We find ourselves trembling. In fact every cell in our body is trembling, for this place is the Holiest of all places; the heart of our God, YHVH. We have pressed through in our worship adventure to enter into this place. We have been invited by the King Himself to enter into His private chambers. We are utterly humbled; we are filled will anticipation.

What will our worship encounter be like here in the Holy of Holies? Can we go in separately or do we enter as the collective Bride of Messiah? This place is unlike the others we have tasted. This place is the smallest so far of all the places of worship though we can barely see anything for the intense light of the Presence of our Creator.

Each worshiper will transcend to the Holy of Holies as the Holy Spirit calls us up into Himself. We will, in this place, enjoy the sweetest intimacy created by our God for His Bride.

Now, let us join the caravan as all God's children enter into His tabernacle. Our first step is to enter into His presence.

All Israel Dances Toward The Tabernacle

Part One

The Outer Court

I

Entering Into the Presence

Have you ever experienced difficulty coming into the presence of our God to worship Him? If your answer is yes, then you are not alone. Often we know we should come to God, but for many reasons we cannot "enter in." But how could we even start by explaining the steps to come into His presence? One by one He has shown us steps to "enter in." The Father shows a lot of emotions when He talks to His people. Yahweh's demonstration of emotions shows me, He places value and time into what He creates.

In this first chapter we will lay a foundation for our sacrifice of worship to our Heavenly Father. The steps are simple to follow. If you occasionally feel your worship is only reaching as high as your ceiling, you will want to check the value and preparation of your heart, your growth and maturity, and the atmosphere of praise and worship. When we enter into the presence of Yahweh, we are a step closer to entering into the Holy of Holies.

Value of the Father

One of the first steps we must take to enter into His presence is to learn how to value our Father. How do we value our relationship

All Israel Dances Toward The Tabernacle

with/to the Father? Or how does the Father value His relationship with/to us? Pondering these two questions we have come up with this conclusion: we can tell what a person values by what they praise. The *Webster's American Dictionary of the English Language* defines value as, to esteem; to hold in respect and estimation; as, to value one for his works or virtues. As human beings do we place value in the King of kings? Or do we merely brush Him aside, and place value in our own selfish desires (Leviticus 27:8,12, Matthew 6:26, 10:31, 12:12, Luke 12:7, 12:24, Colossians 2:23).

As Believers we have a certain lifestyle we must maintain, one that shows value for and commitment to serving our Father. If we present our praise to the Father, then we are placing value into our relationship with Him. It is important people see that we worship Abba. Why is it important people see praise being presented to the Father? The first reason is they will see we place value in our relationship to our God. The second reason is non-believers will come to know our God by our praise. If people see us presenting our praise to the Father, then a question will be raised. "Why do they value their God?"

Human beings only value something that has value to it. What is the value of our God? Mere mortals like us cannot justify the value of our God. We can never know the true value of Him. All we can do is worship Him day in and day out. He is far greater then gold and silver, and His glory extends throughout the heavens. The Father has given us the privilege of continuous worship to Him. By showing value and respect to the king of Kings; He will bless us, and others will want His blessing upon them.

Non-believers in our God will ask themselves "What is their God doing, in order to receive worship and praise?"   When this question is asked, we as believers will show them what our God has done for us. Our God is not some god we take frivolously, but the God of Israel, our Abba. What we praise portrays to others what we value.

From the time we wake up till the time we sleep, the words of Yah should be on our lips. By keeping His words on our mind and lips, it will keep us from sin. If His Living Word is not on our breath continually, are we proclaiming the work of our Father? When He is not in everything we do, then are minds are on the things of the world. To call ourselves Believers in the Father means we will only have His words on our lips. If not we will be living a vain and egotistic reality. This type of reality dilutes the effects of the Father working in our lives. When we reject His all-consuming love, we see He has started a relationship with us. But we've pushed the works of the Father to the side in exchange for our own needs. When we place value and time in our relationship with/to the Father, people will see this, and they will start to know more about the God we worship. This is how we become a witness to people we encounter.

When we praise the Father, we separate ourselves from the rest of the world, rise to our destiny as His called–out people, His royal priesthood (1 Peter 2:9). Just like Abba set Israel apart from the other nations thousands of years ago, we too, the present day house of Israel will be set apart from un-believers. Separating ourselves also illustrates to others that we place value in our relationship with our Heavenly Father. He is the God of Avraham/Abraham, Yitz'chak/Isaac, and Ya'akov/Jacob (Exodus 3:6, 3:15, 1 Kings 18:36, 1 Chronicles 29:18).

Growth and Maturity

Value is very important in the development of the relationship with Yah. When we learn how to respect ourselves by valuing Yah, then we can grow in our relationship to Him. We know what the Father has done for us, now it is time to grow and mature in our praise to Him. If we do not grow and mature in our praise, it is false and shallow. We need to reconstruct our priorities so value can be placed on and time can be allowed for communing with the Divine Presence. Those who witness our praise will see the fruit of the maturing of our relationship. The value of our relationship with the Father will be evident in our praise. How can I do all that the Father would have me to do? This is the question we all should be asking.

When the Father calls us to do His work, will we listen? He could be calling us to a great work, but if we do not grow in Him we will never hear His voice. However, when He calls on us, do we listen? What can we do for our Father? Its simple, just praise and love Him. Praise and Worship will help us grow and mature in our relationship with/to the Father.

The more we get to know someone the more comfortable and intimate we become with that person. Likewise the more we know the Father the more intimate our walk can be with Him. How intimate can our walk be with/to the Father? The closeness one will have with their Abba is up to them. But would it be fair to say most husbands and wives are closer to each other then to their Abba. Abba wants a divine closeness with His people. Some people are not ready yet. The Bride has to be comfortable with the Bridegroom before she consummates her marriage to Him. Abba will continue to work on His relationship with us till we are comfortable with Him. One step at a time, He will take till we completely open our hearts to Him. By experiencing closeness with the Father, we are growing in our praise to Him.

How can we praise something we know nothing about? How can we have a true relationship with the Father if we do not know who He is, and what He has done? As He built our vessels He incorporated the component within all of us to worship Him in numerous ways, including dance. Once we learn how to praise the Father through our song and dance we will be growing and maturing in our Father. As we mature in our praise, we will experience a deeper relationship with him. We will realize He is our ultimate Lover and will wait for the consummation. He is the lover of all lovers. The development of our worship to the Father will only be accomplished by growth and maturity. If we feel our maturing has been halted, we may need to check what our motivation is. Is our praise and worship coming from a pure heart?

Only From A Pure Heart

Having a pure heart means that the motivation within us is directed only at and to the Father. A lot of our actions can come from our heart, but are they *pure*? All actions can come from the heart; but, if our actions are not towards God then it is not of a pure heart. If we pursue hard enough anything we set our mind to, it will be accomplished and will be the fulfillment of the heart. This is how we know if our actions are from the heart. We can tell the purity of our heart by the motivation that drives us from within. If the motivation corresponds to the Living Word then our actions are from a pure heart.

There are times when Believers do not feel the Father's presence around them. They pray and pray and feel nothing. Their life is in shambles and everything around them is going wrong and they don't feel God. Could it be the motivation of their heart is not from God? If you find yourself in this situation you may want to check to see how pure your heart is. We sometimes don't even know the desires of our own heart. Many times I thought my motivation was from God, but it was not. Once I realized my motivation was for my own reasons, I would try and correct it. Realizing my motivation was not from Him brought me into a place of remorse, and emptiness. The emptiness I felt could only be filled with His joy, by my repentance. Through my own selfishness I was restricting my praise to the Father and what He wanted to do for me. This is why it is very important we have a pure heart before the Father. He wants us to walk in His presence with a pure heart.

"I am El Shaddai (God Almighty). Walk in my presence and be pure-hearted" (Genesis 17:1, CJB).

"Create in me a clean heart, O God, and renew a steadfast spirit within me" (Psalms 51:10, NKJV). A clean heart is a heart that has not been defiled from sin, free from contamination. A pure heart is a clean heart before the Father.

Purity of Worship

Can we consider that singing is worship? Can we assume dance is worship? We all have been in a congregational setting when we begin to worship and find our mind would start to wander thinking about other things. As our minds drift and we start to think about worldly things is our praise coming from our pure heart? Dancing and singing, is an outward expression of praise and worship. If our activity of praise and worship is not motivated from a pure heart then it is done in vain. I can dance all I want but if it is not in the purity of my heart then it is not worship and becomes a self-absorbed activity.

What is the Father looking for? He is looking for a heart that is pure. Worship to the Father comes from within us, it is the drive we feel that makes us worship the Father. Praise and worship is embedded into every single soul that has been created. So naturally we all have the desire to bring out the gift of praise and worship Abba has given us. Abba has given us the ability to praise Him with a pure heart. Since we have the ability already then we must use it with pure motivations. The Father will look to see how pure is our praise and worship. Are we ready to have the Father to peek into our heart?

Striving to be pure before the Father is a goal, we all want to reach. Since our Father is perfect in every way, we too will want to be perfect in His sight. Our praise and worship cannot be from a heart of sin but from a clean, pure heart. Why must we strive for perfection? We know the Father is perfect, and we want more of Him, so we must aim to be perfect like Him. The Psalmist in Psalm 119:33 cries out to God to teach him His perfected ways. If I know I can do all I can do for the Father, why would I rob Him of His praise and worship? Abba showed perfection when He created the Heavens and the Earth. His perfected talented work was also used when He created human beings. Without a second thought in His mind, we were created in His likeness. I want to do and be all that I can be for my Abba. This is why we must strive to be perfect in His sight, not man's but Yah's.

The Meaning of Israel

To see that the Father values His people of a pure heart, we will look at the word Israel. The word itself can be dissected into a multitude of definitions. Israel has literal and figurative meanings, along with mystical and abstract ideas. For our purpose we will stick with the literal and mystical meanings of Israel. The *Strong's* gives us the literal meaning. First we will look at *Strong's* #H3478 for Israel: From #H8280 and #H410; he will rule as God; Jisrael, a symbolical name of Jacob; also (typically) of his posterity.

One-way to look at the name Israel is by it's literal meaning. Israel is composed of two words, Sarah and El. Sarah #H8280 - a primitive root; to prevail :-have power (as a prince) and El *Strong's* #H410 - strength; as an adjective mighty, the Almighty, power strong.

Rabbi David A. Copper gives us a mystical definition of the word Israel. "Israel is a code word for that essence in life that longs to be with its Creator." Rabbi Copper derives the word Israel from two words Yashar and El. Yashar *Strong's* #H3474 - to be, go straight, or even, to make right, pleasant prosperous, and direct (the word El is the same as above).

From Rabbi Cooper's definition of Israel, (Yashar) we find there is a connection between the Father and His people. This is one way Israel can be interpreted: "Through Israel, we all have within us a yearning and the direction to return back to the one Who has created us."

This yearning to return to the Father can only happen if we have a heart of purity. Rabbi Copper does an excellent job with his interpretation of the word Israel. I have always had this longing to be with my Creator. The word Israel tells me why.

Israel being the name Yah blessed Ya'acov/Jacob with is the name of purity. (Israel being the name of purity is a picture the Father has shown me. Although this idea may not be accepted, this name of purity is my own interpretation. Other explanations on why Israel is the name of purity will be discussed later in this book.)

Israel's literal meaning (Sarah, El) can be translated as "The one who is mighty and majestic in strength, who will prevail, be prosperous and rule with God." We cannot forget that Israel is also a geographical location in the Middle East. Even though Israel's boundaries are presently receding, it is still the homeland of father Avraham and our ancestors.

Israel is also the symbolic name of Ya'akov. We know Ya'akov was the Father of the twelve tribes of Israel, which became known as the children of Israel. As explained in the Introduction, we are part of Israel, and so we take on this name of purity. This is why it is important to know the meanings of Israel.

Regardless of the different ways Israel can be interpreted, we have to listen to the Father, and allow Him to interpret it for us.

"One will say, 'I belong to the Lord', another will claim himself by the name of Jacob; still another will write on his hand, 'The Lord's,' and will take the name Israel" (Isaiah 44:5, NIV). ("...adopt the surname Isra'el" Complete Jewish Bible.)

A Relationship from Him

The foundation of Israel has been set and we see the Father already has our destiny mapped out. He has our very own lives written into the order of the universe. Our Father is a God of order; He placed order in the stars and the moon. We can safely assume when our Father creates it is part of Him. If creations are from Him, then all His creation is connected to Him and each other. All creation has its rightful place in God's eye and in the universe. With order, stability is established in our universe and is used for our Father's plan. Abba started His relationship with us before we were born into this world. The Father starts the relationship first, by His creation of humans.

By starting His relationship with us before we were born, He reveals that He places value into the relationships, which He created. Relationships are not the responsibility of a single participant; rather it involves an intimate closeness between two recipients who are willing to blend in oneness of minds. Abba has already taken up His part of the relationship; now it is our turn to respond to that call, to be Echad (one) with the Father (Ecclesiastes 12:7).

Atmosphere of Praise and Worship

As we prepare our hearts to be surrounded by the presence of Yahweh, it is an act of our will to enter into an inspiring relationship with Him. This is the first step that we must take to enter in His relationship. As Humans, we have the choice to enter into the atmosphere of praise and worship. The Father has given us a freewill, to do whatever we like. With our free will comes a constant pulling of evil forces trying to work within and against us. The evil will try to stir our thoughts and emotions, and turn us from the Father. Freewill depends on the existence of evil. Without evil, would we still have a choice of serving Yah or Satan? If evil did not exist then we would only serve our Father. But our Father gave us free will– a choice. There are only two choices from which to choose, good or evil. This is why we have this struggle within ourselves.

Earthly beings are the only ones who have the choice to enter within His atmosphere. Heavenly beings are already wrapped in His glory and they do not have the constant decision of choosing right from wrong.

The atmosphere of praise and worship is the Father's Spirit surrounding and protecting us. It is important that we all enter into this atmosphere and allow the Father to surround us. If we look at the Earth's atmosphere, we find there is a mass of fluid, consisting of air, and aqueous vapors. This mass surrounds the earth and protects it from the harsh forces of the universe. Therefore, the main purpose of the Earth's atmosphere is to protect. In the same way, the Father's Spirit surrounds us and we are covered by His protection.

We have the choice to enter or not to enter into the Father's atmosphere of praise and worship. We need to strain to reach for that higher level with the Father, stepping into a new life, and leaving the old behind. It is a decision of our own will to enter into the atmosphere of praise and worship created by the presence of God. Once we enter into this place the Father has planned for us, we will see the difference living in this atmosphere can make in our life. We will see true and everlasting love, which can only come from the Father of heavenly lights.

The Presence of Yahweh

Entering into the Presence of Yahweh is the most magnificent event we can partake in. By "entering" we know the Father has accepted us, and allowed us to come into His presence. His presence is like nothing else on earth. When we value Abba, He in-turn values us. He will be there knocking at our door showing us the path to return to Him. Once we are on the path to return, we can grow and mature in His ways. He wants us to return but will we allow Him to help us to return?

Growing and maturing is vital to our relationship with Him. If we do not grow in Him then we will never be able to reach the atmosphere of praise and worship. We want to reach the atmosphere of praise and worship so we can get to know the Father more. Knowing the Father more will allow us to experience a closer walk with Him, so He can minister and talk to us. When we do reach His atmosphere, He has allowed us to enter, meaning we are coming to Him with a pure heart. The gates will be open for us to enter into the presence of Yahweh.

We are just at the foot gate of the outer court of the tabernacle. Let us press on till we get into the Holy of Holies. Once inside the Holy of Holies our minds can vaguely comprehend what the Father has for us. He waits for our arrival!

All Israel Dances Toward The Tabernacle

2

I'd Love to Dance, If I Only Knew How!

If you think you cannot dance, you are not alone. "I'd love to dance if I only knew how!" is the common response we hear when we invite someone to dance in worship. The reason most of us think this way is because we believe we have two left feet, or we imagine we have no sense of rhythm. Finally, we think we cannot dance because we do not know the steps. In our mind-set, or way of thinking, these are socially acceptable excuses for not dancing. Let us take a look at what our Heavenly Father means when He speaks of dance.

Contrasting Ideas

"Joy is gone from our hearts; our dancing has turned to mourning" (Lamentations 5:15, NIV).

"...a time to weep and a time to laugh, a time to mourn and a time to dance" (Ecclesiastes 3:4, NIV).

"You turned my wailing into dancing; you removed my sackcloth and clothed me with joy (KJV, gladness), that my heart may sing to you and not be silent. O LORD my God, I will give you thanks forever" (Psalms 30:11-12, NIV).

Just what is dance? To answer this question we look to David Stern to help us understand the workings of Hebrew poetry. His explanation of the usage of Hebrew poetry enables us to grasp the intent of the authors of the verses above. In Stern's translation of the *Complete Jewish Bible*, his introduction on pages xxxi and xxxii is cited; "About 30% of the Tanakh [Old Testament] is written in the form of poetry ... The key to Biblical Hebrew poetry is not primarily rhythm, but parallelism. The poetry is divided usually into one of three [parts] things: it [the line] expresses essentially the same idea as the first [line] or it presents a contrasting idea, or it adds to the first line's thought."

First, let's look at a few Hebrew word definitions. *Strong's* word for dance in Lamentations 5:15 is #H7540 raqad (raw-kad') a primitive root; to stamp; example, to spring about (wildly or for joy): -dance, jump, leap, skip.

The word for dance in the Psalms and Ecclesiastes verses from above is #H4234 machowl (maw-khole); a round dance: dance (-cing). From 2342 chuwl; (pronounced kool) - twist or whirl, dance ... plus lots more.

The word for mourn is #H5594 caphad (saw-fad') a primitive root; to tear the hair and beat the breasts (as Orientals do in grief); generally to lament; by implication to wail: -lament, mourn (-er), wail.

We can see from Ecclesiastes 3:4 that laughing is contrasting weeping. Joy, in Lamentations 5:15 is #H4885 masows (maw-soce'); delight; or the feeling of joy, mirth, rejoice. From #H7797 - suws (soos) primitive root; to be bright, cheerful; -be glad, greatly, joy, make mirth, rejoice.

Gladness #H8057 simchah (sim-khaw'); blithesomeness or glee, exceeding gladness, joy (-fullness), pleasure, rejoicing.

Dancing is the opposite of mourning according to the Biblical meaning. Webster's defines mourning as the act of sorrowing especially for a person's death; lamentation; the customary exhibition of grief for the death of a person; also, the period of so doing. To mourn is to express or to feel grief or sorrow; to grieve; lament, to show the customary tokens of grief for the death of someone, to utter in a mournful manner. Antonyms of mourn are exult, rejoice, celebrate, delight, cheer, and glory.{cool, huh!}

We see from the definitions that mourning is an act; it is something we show or demonstrate. In other words, it is a manifestation of what we are feeling. The contrast to mourn will also be something we show. Does anyone need to be taught how to mourn? Some cultures are taught to bottle up emotions. Demonstrating sorrow can be a social expression, or the gesture can come out from our inner most being. It can be un-learned or learned.

In Ecclesiastes, weeping parallels with mourning and laughing parallels with dancing. We see from this brief word study that dance is the opposite of mourning. The Biblical definition for dance therefore is the expression of joy.

Weeping / mourning is opposite of laughing /dancing.

Dance is Joy

It is interesting to note that the Ruach/Spirit did not word the Lamentation verse (above) like this; "You have turned my dancing into standing still." Is not this what some seem to think is being said? If we stop dancing, we are standing still, not moving. Right?

When joy is removed, dancing has been removed. If there is no joy, there can be no dancing. Dancing is the manifestation of joy.

In the book of Lamentations we find the nation of Israel hanging up their harps. She could no longer sing praises unto her Yah. She was unable to express joy. This was evident because she no longer danced. When our dancing is turned into mourning, we stop dancing. Today we are seeing the joy of the LORD returning to Yah's people and with joy comes the restoration of the dance. The restoration cannot be stopped. Dance is the expression of joy. Although we may express our joy in different ways, the Biblical definition for joy is dance.

"Because you did not serve the LORD your God JOYFULLY and gladly in the time of prosperity, therefore in hunger and thirst, in nakedness and dire poverty, you will serve the enemies the LORD sends against you. He will put an iron yoke on your neck until he has destroyed you" (Deuteronomy 28:47-48, NIV).

If we are serving our Yah with JOY, dance will become a natural expression of that joy. If we are not serving with JOY then the enemy will defeat us. This is scary to think about. Have we ever heard teachings about why the enemy is defeating us? Could the simple reason be that we are not serving our Yah with joy?! To serve our Yah by expressing His joy through dance could be the answer to all of our world problems. Think of the possibilities!

Like Father Like Son

Joy is the emotion excited by the acquisition or expectation of good; gladness; delight; state of happiness; bliss; that which causes happiness (*Webster's*).

We have heard it said from pulpits, books, teaching tapes and other sources that our Yah is not emotional. Yet, did He not create us with emotions? If one of the characteristics of the fruit of the Spirit (Galatians 5:22) is JOY, then we can safely enjoy (no pun intended!) the JOY of the LORD!! How can an orange be the fruit from an orange tree unless it is the color orange? If it came off the tree in blue, we would not want to eat this 'orange.' So, the fruit of the spirit has certain characteristics, one being JOY. As Yah's people, we will have joy, for joy is of Him. He has joy, for we find in Nehemiah 8:10 that "the joy of the LORD is our strength." His joy strengthens us to accomplish the tasks He calls us to do for His glory.

Like Father, like son. The Father's children will behave like Him and have the same characteristics; in this case, JOY. A friend once told me, " If you have joy, you have it all. You will have peace, hope, health, faith ... everything!" I ponder this often. Even though the circumstances are less than ideal (and I know each of us are experiencing challenges), if we lean on His joy, we will be strong. A word to the wise; "Don't let the enemy rob your joy!"

Joy Bubbles

Should you have the opportunity to visit the Lake of the Ozarks in Missouri, you must stop by one of the National Parks there called Ha Ha Tonka. Ha Ha Tonka is a beautiful state park, full of walking trails, old majestic shade trees and panoramic views. This huge park is named for the spring waters, which have been flowing there for hundreds of years. It is a cool walk, even in summer, down the long path to arrive at the water's edge. I love to go to natural parks to commune with the Creator of such beauty. When I go to Ha Ha Tonka I like to pray and enjoy its tranquility. On one occasion I read the park's information board. To my delight I discovered that the name of the park was an Indian word, which meant, "laughing waters." Needless to say, I laughed at the picture I had in my head of Native Americans enjoying this beautiful place and receiving (from the Creator) the name Ha Ha Tonka. In this case, the name was given which described the source of many natural springs. In essence, the moving, living waters were laughing waters. This name gives us a picture of the Holy Spirit Who is bubbling up from the inside of us. He is the source of joy. He is the Living Water (John 7:38).

While dancing at one event, I got so full of joy I could not stop laughing! I kept dancing and laughing; just giggling like a little child. It was a most wonderful experience of which I had never had before – simply delightful. That kind of joy is what I call, "joy bubbles." To me, when this happens, it seems like bubbles come to the surface and pop, thereby producing the giggle (it tickles). This reminds me of children dancing and playing and laughing before their father. In our case, we are dancing and playing before our Abba.

Get Alone and Express Yourself!

You might be saying, "Well I just don't dance, it's not for me and besides, I'm too self-conscious." The ideal place to begin to dance before our God is in the privacy of our room where no one except He is watching. Here is where we can become comfortable expressing our inner most feelings, which we may not easily verbalize. All of our emotions may be expressed through dance; our society or culture places no restrictions on us in our room. In our privacy, we may express sadness, frustrations, even anger, as well as joy and thanksgiving.

If you have His joy in your heart, you can dance. You need not be concerned about right foot and left foot. You need not have to focus on the up beat or the downbeat. Don't worry about the waltz, the cha cha or swing. Simply put on your favorite worship tape and start moving. It's that easy, and fun. Look at you, You're dancing!

Soon, when Abba knows you are ready, He will invite you to dance with Him in public worship setting. Here, all Yah's children will, one day, have the freedom and confidence to dance before Him. The time is coming when the chairs will be removed from our houses of worship, allowing a large area for all to join in the dance. Praising and worshiping our Yah in the public worship setting has an anointing so sweet and overwhelming; it is sweeter than any wine! Don't hold back from offering your dance as a living sacrifice to Him in the congregation. It may be the very thing to set someone else free to worship Him.

As the restoration of all things comes to its completion, we will see more and more dancing. Some people are trying to stop this restoration. But it cannot be stopped, anymore than any man can stop the prophetic Word of God from its fulfillment. As the two sticks come together in Abba's hand (Ezekiel 37), we will see the virgins coming in the dance, old men and young together.

"Then maidens will dance and be glad, young men and old as well. I will turn their mourning into gladness; I will give them comfort and joy instead of sorrow" (Jeremiah 31:13, NIV). {Notice again the Hebrew parallelism?}

"I will build you up again and you will be rebuilt, O Virgin Israel. Again you will take up your tambourines and go out to dance with the joyful" (Jeremiah 31:4, NIV).

"He Turned My Mourning Into Dancing"

I'd like to share what happened to me at a memorial service for a baby. When I received the report that a baby in my congregation died, I sensed the prompting of the Ruach that I was to dance at the memorial service. Encouraged by the peace in my heart that this prompting to dance was from Him, I obtained permission from the leadership and the parents who were very receptive. Having no experience in this ministry setting, I prayed diligently to obtain clear direction from God. The dance was to be called, "He turned my mourning into dancing."

He steered me to the specific music and dance garments. No selection of music I owned seemed to fit the occasion except for several instrumental pieces. I finally settled on a few instrumentals. The mourning scarf I used in the beginning of the dance, transformed into a garment of praise at the end, was tied around my waist. Drawn to wear a certain shirt proved to be the sensitive direction of the LORD as well. The Creator of Heavenly Lights orchestrated every detail about this dance including the choice of music and the clothing which I would wear.

Not knowing if I could complete the dance without crying and being nervous, His Spirit empowered me to carry out the dance without any pre-planned choreography or rehearsal. As I ran down the aisle at the end, He impressed me to tie the praise scarf on the baby's mom!

Many were crying as the Spirit of Comfort ministered to the mourners. After dancing at the memorial service, Abba ministered to me more than any prior dance. Many told me of how the dance ministered to them; down to the choice of dance garments! Later the grandmother told me she had seen a figurine of a woman holding a baby dressed exactly as I was clothed for the dance. She had bought the figurine for her daughter, the mom of the baby, earlier that morning. I believe this dance was the most special and unique dance I have ever accomplished. The Ruach's creativity is endless. We need to allow Him to be all He wants to be through us.

Final Steps

The title of this chapter was spoken to me while worshiping at a feast of the LORD. The sister was all smiles as she danced before her God in the dance circle. She didn't think she was good enough. She told me, "I'd love to dance if I only knew how!" We are so hard on ourselves, aren't we? Let's remember we are not called to be professional worshipers. We are called to offer our bodies a living sacrifice. To one person that passage may mean one thing and to another it may mean something quite different. Perhaps some days we have pain in our bodies, or we are depressed. These situations can hold us back from offering our sacrifice. Don't be too hard on yourself. Move what you can and if that is a sacrifice from a pure heart, Abba will accept it with delight.

Have you seen athletes run without legs, or play basketball paralyzed from the waist down? If we want to do something badly enough, we will find a way to do it. I have seen worshipers who are on crutches dance and worshipers in wheel chairs dance (a paraplegic, to be specific). Now what is your excuse?

The final steps of this dance (in this chapter) are only the beginning for your personal dance/worship time with your God. You have seen that dance in our Father's eyes is not what dance is in the eyes of our society or culture. You are now armed with the simple 'how to' dance for the King. You have examples of how the Ruach can minister in dance in unique settings. Now, shall we dance?

All Israel Dances Toward The Tabernacle

I'd Love To Dance...

3

The Beginning of Dance

Yahweh "formed a person [Hebrew: Adam] from the dust of the ground [Hebrew: adamah] and breathed into his nostrils the breath of life, so that he became a living being" (Genesis 2:7, CJB).

Breath of Life

Let us examine how "dance" became part of worship. Genesis 2:7 tell us Yahweh created a person from dust and with His Spirit gave life to the individual. When the first human, was formed, Abba left him without life, or void. The way in which Yahweh created man, or breathed life into man is parallel to the way in which Yahweh created the Earth.

Before Yah spoke creation into existence, His Spirit hovered over the surface of the waters and there was void and darkness (Genesis 1:2). The word "Spirit" comes from *Strong's* #H7307 – ruach (roo-akh).

Ruach means wind, by resemblance of breath, (figuratively) life, anger, and mind (more). Its root word is #H7306 meaning to blow, breathe; only (literally) to smell or (by implication.) perceive (figuratively to anticipate, enjoy); - accept, smell, touch, make of quick understanding.

Then Yahweh said, "Let there be light" with that creation begun to unfold, by the breath from which He spoke. Furthermore on the sixth day of His creating Yah spoke again, sending His Spirit into His creation, giving man life (Genesis 1:11,14,20,24,26, 2 Corinthians 5:1). Now we can see the parallel between the creation of the Earth and the creation of man. *Strong's* number for "breathed" in Genesis 2:7 is #H5397. The Hebrew word used is "nshamah" (nesh-aw-maw) meaning puff, soul, spirit, or divine inspiration, wind and intellect. Nshamah's root word is #H5395 nasham (naw-sham) meaning to blow away, destroy. From the Hebrew word "nshamah" we see that Yah gave the man a soul/spirit.

As there was no life-giving Spirit in the individual, Yah breathed into the nostrils of the man, sending His Spirit (which gives life). Therefore we have a part of the Father dwelling in us twenty-four hours a day (Genesis 2:7, Job 27:3). He placed a Part of Himself into us. His "life force" became part of man, giving man a desire to praise the Father. Just by the man's existence there was praise circulating to Abba.

From the creation of man, we see how praise and worship, including dance and singing, came into existence. Since we all are temples of the Holy Spirit, Part of the Father dwells in us (1 Corinthians 6:19-20). Our soul/spirit is a Part of the Father, which gives us the connection to be one with Him. Our soul/spirit is a Part of the Father that gives us the desire to praise, worship and bow down to the Almighty Creator. Our soul/spirit is a Part of God and is His eternal breath. Abba made us from His image and likeness so we can be like Him (Genesis 1:26).

Moshe's God

Let's look at Moshe leading the people of Israel out from Egypt after hundreds of years of bondage. Exodus 15 starts out by proclaiming praise to the Father. Moshe makes a list of qualities about His God, from His strength to His salvation, to His mighty Name. Moshe really knew who His God was. He records one quality after another about who his God is and what He had done for him and the people of Israel (verse 2). "This is my God," Moshe declares with pride. We do not claim ownership to something unless we value it. Moshe valued his God. A mighty relationship is being established between Moshe and Yah. Moshe placed value into this relationship, which he had with the Father. "With a blast from Your nostrils the waters piled up – the water stood up like a wall" (verse 8, CJB). Verse eight takes us back to Genesis 2:7; with the same Spirit of life comes destruction (remember the definition for breathed above). We see with the same Spirit that Yah used to create life He also used to destroy it.

Introducing Miryam

The first time the word "dance" is mentioned in scripture is in Exodus 15:20. "Also Miryam/Miriam the prophet, sister of Aharon/Aaron, took a tambourine in her hand; and all the women went out after her with tambourines, dancing" (Exodus 15:20, CJB). Why is Miryam such an important person in the development of dance as praise and worship? What made her so special that she would be known chiefly for her dance and her praise? The Torah (first five books of the Bible) gives Miryam certain qualities making her a respected person in the eyes of Israel. Let us look a little closer at Miryam so that we can better understand who she is, and her significant role as a dancer.

Miryam is a prophetess (Hebrew: nbiy'ah (neb-ee-yaw) *Strong's* #H5031). She is an inspired women or champion of Yah. Her name is Mir-yam, which means bitterness. She was born into the tribe of Levi, a priestly tribe, or the called out ones (1 Chronicles 15:2). As the people of Israel entered the Zin desert, they stayed in Kadesh. Kadesh is where Miryam (daughter of Amram and Joehebed) died and was buried (Numbers 20:1). *Nelson's Illustrated Bible Dictionary* states that the region of Kadesh is known for the event when Israel rebelled against Yah's appointed leaders. Miryam was a leader of the people (Micah 6: 4), and at the same time was utilized as an example by Yahweh (Deuteronomy 24:9).

Let us summarize what we know about Miryam:

◆ prophetess (Exodus 15:20, Jasher 68:1; see note at the end of this chapter on the book of Jasher)
◆ born into priestly tribe (Exodus 15:20)
◆ dancer, singer, poet (Exodus 15:20-21)
◆ an example (Deuteronomy 24:9)
◆ leader of the people (Micah 6:4)
◆ greatly respected by the people (Numbers 12:5-10)

Read the above scriptures before you move on. For they explain her personality. Miryam was hand picked by Yah to lead His people. The Bible does not state when her job was completed. Miryam's job did not end when she died. In fact her work is just beginning. She has become the leader, in a frontier, which, in spirit, she will show us to dance before Abba. Now that we better understand who Miryam is we return to Exodus 15:20.

"Also Miryam the prophet, sister of Aaron took a tambourine in her hand; and all the women went out after her with tambourines, and dancing" (Exodus 15:20, CJB).

First Dance in Scripture

Dance is first mentioned in conjunction with tambourines in Exodus 15:20. The Hebrew word for dance in this verse is mechowlah (mekh-o-law), *Strong's* #H4246. Toph (tofe), *Strong's* #H8596, is the Hebrew word for tambourine. The type of dance Miryam and the other women were doing was a circle or round dance. We know this because in Hebrew mechowlah means round or circle dance, or even a dance company. Miryam's dance can be demonstrated as an acceptable offering to the Father. Her sacrifice is an offering of gratitude and thankfulness. For Yah has just destroyed the Egyptians and has answered their prayers. After the crossing of the sea, Israel thanked God by singing and dancing. These expressions of praise are natural human emotions. We all have these emotions deep within us. When we allow ourselves to be open, these feelings will be released enabling us to reach a new level of understanding of Who and What the Father is.

The next verse, Exodus 15:21, goes into a song Miryam was singing while she was dancing with her tambourine. "Sing to Yah, for He is highly exalted! The horse and its rider He threw in the sea!" (CJB). This verse is one of the earliest forms of Hebrew poetry.

If we will play a game of connect the dots, we can see that the Father has placed several dots in a row for us, and all we have to do is connect them. We see Miryam doing her victory dance after the crossing of the sea (this is the first dot). At the same time she also sang to the children of Israel (the second dot). Now we connect the two dots and we see a different picture has been revealed. Dancing and singing go hand in hand as we offer our sacrifice of worship to the Father.

Miryam did not just sing, or just dance, but she participated in both forms of worship at the same time. Miryam was a prophet of Yah, and He entrusted her to lead His people. If it was acceptable for Yah to model the people after Miryam, then surely it is acceptable, for us to follow her example as well. Wouldn't you agree?

Miryam as a Leader

Exodus 15:20 shows us of the influence Miryam had over the people, "All the women went out after her." She was the leader, the rest were followers. Miryam showed how dance, song, tambourines and praise, were all acceptable offerings to the

Father. She was chosen by Yah to be a leader and an authority figure to the people of Israel (Micah 6:4).

Miryam did more than just dance. She was the one who brought forth the prophecy, concerning her parents birthing a son who then would deliver them from Egypt (Jasher 68:1 see note at end of chapter). Being a prophet of Yah, when Miryam spoke, people listened. In Numbers 12:5-10, Miryam was struck down with a sickness for rebuking Moshe for marrying an Egyptian woman; then she was cast out of the camp for seven days.

The remarkable event about this story is all the people of Israel waited until she was healed and returned before they continued on their journey to the Promised Land. Millions and millions of people waited until she was healed. The story then tells us she was healed through the intercession of Moshe.

When Yah delivered the nation, Israel was so excited all they could do was sing and dance. But why? Dancing unto Abba with song was a way they could outwardly express their emotions. The miraculous event was probably more like an explosion, a fire that was burning deep within! Something in them made them so passionate about their God they had no choice but to bow down and dance before the Almighty. As a unified people they rose up together to meet their destiny. This shows us the value of Miryam as a leader of Israel.

Diffusion is the Simple Solution

Another way we could look at praise, worship and dance is through the scientific term of diffusion. Diffusion – random motion, scatters molecules evenly or diffusely, within a given volume. Or something of a higher concentration flowing to a lower concentration. When we hear a song that inspires us and we want to dance, we can look at this feeling as diffusion. Could we say that the Father sends these molecules of energy (aka. Holy Spirit) from the music to filtrate through the whole body? When this happens, a change effect occurs throughout the soul/spirit, energizing us to worship the Father. The Holy Spirit flows from the higher concentration (God) to a lower concentration (man).

Lenny and Varda Harris, of *Adonai Echad* and *Renah!* fame, are praise and worship warriors for the Almighty Yah! Every time we hear their music, it sets us into a different motion. As we are worshiping it seems there are invisible molecules of energy (aka. Holy Spirit), sent by their music, that enters our mind. From there it is diffused throughout our body. After this type of diffusion takes place, the intense feelings and emotions are gathered together, ready to be released. The over-bearing energy gets released, either by singing, dancing, or even falling on our face before Yah.

The awesome part of this scenario is when praise energy is released into the air something happens. The praise energy helps create an atmosphere of praise and worship, not so much for the individual anymore, but for the outsider looking in. This idea of praise can be looked upon as a "recyclable flow of energy." While the atmosphere is being positioned around us the Spirit changes everything and sets the tone for worship. Now we have the "praise energy" or the Holy Spirit, which is encamped around the heavens and the earth, praising the Almighty Creator.

"The heavens declare the glory of Yah, the dome of the sky speaks the work of His hands. Every day it utters speech, every night it reveals knowledge. Without speech, without a word, without their voices being heard, their line goes out through all the earth and their words to the end of the world" (Psalms 19:11, CJB).

Recyclable Flow of Praise Energy

The above example of diffusion shows how prophetess Miryam used the recyclable flow of "praise energy" so the people of Israel would follow. Miryam was probably the first one to ignite this miraculous event. She was the ignition who started the flow of the "electrical system" of the Holy Spirit. Now the atmosphere has been prepared, with the Spirit just blazing out of her. The Spirit of Yah became so heavy that the other "temples" (we are the present day tabernacle/temple that the Holy Spirit dwells in twenty-four hours a day, 1 Corinthians 6:19-20) in which the Spirit dwelt began to react. With the above thought in mind, we have the other women reacting to the atmosphere that Miryam had established. This is like the congregation being lead into the atmosphere of praise and worship through the praise and worship leaders. Now we see how Miryam became a leader of the people (Micah 6:4). Praise to the all mighty Yahweh, who is Adonai Tzva'ot the Lord of Hosts!

The Creator begins and ends this process. He sends His Spirit down to the man. The man then uses the Spirit as "praise energy." When the Spirit is released, the Spirit goes back to the Creator. But the Creator also sends His Spirit back to man, therefore making this a continual cycle. Who can explain our limitless God, Who is everywhere and in everything?! The recyclable flow of "praise energy" is my own interpretation on how the Holy Spirit sparks us in praise. (The above interpretation was from a vision, which I perceived was from the Father. "For from Him and through Him and to Him are all things" [Romans 11:36, CJB].)

Miryam and the Book of Jasher

Miryam is only mentioned in the Holy Scriptures a dozen times. Here are excerpts from the book of Jasher, telling of Miryam's prophecy.

"And it was at that time that the Spirit of Yah was upon Miryam the daughter of Amram, the sister of Aaron. She went forth with prophecies about the house, saying: Behold a son will be born unto us from my father and mother at this time. He will save Israel from the lands of Egypt."

-32-

"And Miryam his sister (referring to Moshe) called him Jered, for she descended after him to the river to know what his end would be."

"Miryam wanted to know what would become of her words, so she watched as the child was set into the river." (also in Exodus 1:4)

Note:

The above verses are taken from the book of Jasher chapter 68:1,14,21 which book of Jasher was translated into English from Hebrew. Our Holy Scriptures validates this book (*The book of Jasher*, pg. 202-203, Artisan Sales, 1988): "Is not this written in the book of Jasher" (Joshua 10:13, TSET). And, "Behold, it is written in the book of Jasher" 2 Samuel 1:18, TSET).

Our foundation in dance, as praise and worship will continue to grow as we seek the Father. Let us continue our journey of restoration and celebration, which we partake of in the restoration of the arts!

All Israel Dances Toward The Tabernacle

4

Restoration of the Arts

Gifts of Old.

A certain sister was introduced as a poet. I sat in my seat to wait for her sweet poetry thinking, "This will be 'nice.'" The minute she began to speak, I had to repent to the Father for pre-judging her and her beautiful gift from Him. The poem He had inspired captured the entire audience. We sat spell-bound. Not only did she speak a message from the throne, but also she delivered it with action, pantomime, and a voice filled with passion and fire. I had never experienced anything like it. This was an awesome gift.

Later, I spoke with her as she gave the Father all the credit for this lost art. She humbly told me of the ninety year old gentleman who wrote her a letter the years after he had heard her present one of her poems. The delivery of her poem haunted him all those years and he just had to write her to let her know he had finally turned his will over to His Savior. This gift of the Heavenly Bridegroom had eternal fruit for His kingdom.

As Abba restores Israel, He will, in turn, restore all the gifts to us, that we might help advance His Kingdom and His family.

"I have also spoken to [you by] the prophets, and I have multiplied visions [for you] and [have appealed to you] through parables acted out by the prophets" (Hosea 12:10, Amplified).

"I have also spoken by the prophets and I have multiplied visions and used similitudes by the ministry of the prophets" (Hosea 12:10, KJV).

The literal translation uses the word, likenesses.

Similitude is an old King James word. *Strong's* #H1819 - damah (daw-maw') a primitive root; to compare; by implication to resemble, liken, consider: - compare, devise, (be) like (-n), mean, think, use similitudes.

Webster defines similitude as similarity; resemblance. A simile. A parable. An allegory. One that is like or similar; a facsimile. Semblance; form.

A Picture is Worth a Thousand Words

Our fabulous Father created us with emotions and senses. These special faculties of sensation enable us to experience His world in depth. Our five senses of sight, hearing, smell, touch, and taste enable us to encounter and enjoy Him as well. Have you noticed the many word-pictures there are in His Instructional Guide to us? The Bible is full of parables and word-pictures. Wouldn't you agree we readily remember these word-pictures? Yes we do. And our Father uses them because He knows how to communicate with us.

The prophet Yechezk'el/Ezekiel delivered twenty-five pantomimes to YHVH's people. He didn't merely vocalize the prophecy; he acted out the message. We can place ourselves in the sandals of the to-be-exiled nation of Israel and know they must have lain in their beds at night with pictures of Yechezk'el acting out his latest skit going through their heads.

Yechezk'el is not the only mimist. Can we forget Yesha'yahu/Isaiah in chapter twenty? How would you like to be the one Father tells to walk naked and barefoot for three years? Yirmryahu/Jeremiah is credited with seven pantomimes and Hoshea/Hosea offers three besides the one mentioned above.

Rehearsed vs. Spontaneous

Haven't we all been guilty of putting our Heavenly Father in a box? Is it time to repent? Let Him come out of the box! Let's enjoy Him to our fullest potential. Our limitations cannot be allowed to limit Him. He is Unlimited! Not in my wildest dreams did I think I could be ministered to by a poem. But I was wrong.

Dance, as a form of ministry to Yah's people, is experiencing a restoration. Not all houses of worship will allow dance to be expressed as praise and worship, yet. However, more and more Believers are feeling a stirring in their spirits that is making them want to dance. However, dance, as a mode of delivering a message to Yah's people will be restored. The more we allow the arts to return into our houses of worship, the more we will be able to worship Him in spirit and truth. The more we allow the arts to come back into our houses of worship, the more completely we will be able to know Him.

Many a time I have heard the 'song of the LORD' come forth in congregational worship settings. Often this type of spontaneous song will move me to weeping and falling on my face to adore the I AM. The delivery of the message is not the important issue here. The message and the response are the important things. If Yechezk'el's pantomimes did not prick the people's hearts and convict them of their wayward ways, he would have failed.

Spontaneous dance can have the same effect on Yah's people. The song comes to our hearing and the dance comes to our sight. Spontaneous music coming from an instrument of praise can also have a moving effect in our spirits. All can be used effectively by our Father to 'say' something to the congregation. The lasting picture will remain.

We have enjoyed music, song and dance as mediums to deliver a message from our Father. We call rehearsed presentations that are inspired by the Ruach/Spirit, "Spirit-led." Spontaneous music coupled with spontaneous song, joined with spontaneous dance will deliver a powerful message from the throne. Whether rehearsed or spontaneous, both can minister when inspired by Father's Spirit.

As we witness the restoration of the House of David, musicians and dancers will be working together to minister to Yah's people. Both must be prepared to 'step' out into this renewed space allowing Ruach to express His heart. Too long we have had the mind-set of encountering Father from a neck up and eye closed posture. Let us open our eyes during corporate worship times. Let us open all our senses to Him, the Creator of those senses.

"Taste and see that the LORD is good; blessed is the man who takes refuge in him" (Psalm 34:8, NIV).

"Like an apple tree among the trees of the forest is my lover among the young men. I delight to sit in his shade, and his fruit is sweet to my taste" (Song of Songs, NIV).

In the Song of Songs, the Beloved Shulamite is intoxicated with the fragrance of her Lover, which is likened to the intoxicating effects of sweet wine. See chapter One of the Song of Songs.

The Blind Pianist

During a time of congregational praise and worship, the blind pianist, Pat, began to play on her piano music, which I perceived was unrehearsed. The desire in me to dance was overwhelming. I began to move with the swirls of the music. I thought to myself, "This is the most wonderful experience ever!" I could not comprehend what was going on but I knew it was of God! She and I flowed together like we had rehearsed the number for months. After what seemed like hours, I sensed the end of the music coming. For a moment I panicked. I was not able to communicate with Pat to let her know I was finished. My inexperience soon melted away in renewed confidence. We both ended exactly at the same time!

Postscript of Wisdom

While obedience to the prompting of Ruach Elohim/Spirit of God is foremost, we need to also be obedient to leaders He has placed within His Body. Abba taught me through Todd Farley, an anointed and talented mime-dancer, how to communicate in the spontaneous setting. He offered me sound Godly advice that I have made routine in my ministry.

Arrive to praise and worship prepared to dance with proper shoes and dress.

Prior to the start of the meeting clearly communicate with the leadership, such as the MC or worship leader. Inform them you are ready to minister in spontaneous dance if the Spirit should prompt.

Secure his/her blessing; accept instructions as to the space in which you may use to deliver the dance, etc.

One final note of encouragement; when the music starts and your heart is pounding, don't drag your feet through the whole song waiting for the right moment to step out there! Numerous times this very thing has happened to me. I have kicked myself all the way home and vowed never to let an opportunity like that slip past me again. Songs are only a few minutes long. Once it is over, it is over. We cannot go up to the worship leader and say, "God gave me a dance for that song, can you play it again?"

Ministers in the Arts! Get ready to move into space Abba has prepared for you from the foundations of His world! Exercise those gifts to glorify the Giver. As the entire house of Israel is re-united, let us desire to drink in the 'whole meggilah'!

All Israel Dances Toward The Tabernacle

Restoring The Arts

Part Two

The Inner Court

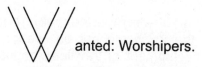

5

The Dancing Warrior

Wanted: Worshipers.

Having picked up a catalogue I had received in the mail, I was going to toss it in the trash when the word, 'dance' caught my eye. The caption read, "Spiral Dance 288pp. rituals, exercises and magic. Eloquent and brilliant overview of the growth, suppression and re-emergence of Witchcraft as a Goddess religion. A classic. Revised edition."

I was shocked to read this ad. Are you? It is an interesting ad in light of a question that is often put to me: "Is dance as warfare new?"

Dance has been around for along time. However, we believe that what we want to bring forth is a new understanding of an old Scriptural tradition.

The power in/of dance goes beyond our wildest imagination. If we say we understand it all, we are only fooling ourselves. Whether you are experienced in dance or a new comer, we hope to reveal some long hidden truths about worship and, specifically dance.

Part One

A). Army of Dancing Angels

Review the passage where Ya'akov/Jacob leaves his father-in-law, Lavan/Laban, in Genesis 31.

Early in the morning Lavan got up, kissed his sons and daughters, and blessed them. Then Lavan left and returned to his own place. Ya'akov went on his way, and the angels of God met him. When Ya'akov saw them, he said, "This is God's camp," and called that place Machanayim [two camps] (Genesis 32:1-3, CJB).

This word Mahanaim (makh-an-eh-yim) note the spelling in most other translations is without the y, should not be overlooked. *Strong's* #4264 - literal an encampment of travelers, troops, or figuratively of dancers, stars, etc. The root word, #H2583 khawnaw (khaw-naw), means to incline, rest in a tent.

When Ya'akov saw God's messengers, what did he see? The translators of our Bibles do a wonderful job, don't they? It is a tough assignment. Hebrew is a beautiful language. I am no Hebrew scholar and rely on *Strong's* Concordance for grasping the meanings of certain words. For one Hebrew word the translators often have a dozen or more words from which to choose. When we select a different word for a definition rather than the commonly accepted one, we see a changed picture. It will take the Spirit of our Father to open our understanding to new possibilities. We want to see our Father from ever facet of His personality, don't we?

B. The Army of Yah

Webster's definition of army = a body of persons organized to advance a cause; a great number; host; array. {army does not refer to combat} host - a great multitude, a throng

Strong's #6635 is host - a mass of servants, organized, by implication, for worship, (more).

Webster's definition of array:
1 - to dispose in order, as troops; marshal.
2 - to deck; to adorn with dress; envelop.
(array as a noun)
1 - order; a regular and imposing arrangement.
2 - a whole body of persons placed in order.
3 - rich or beautiful apparel.

For years, even centuries, we Believers have seen ourselves in the military or 'army' of God. We call ourselves soldiers, we speak of going to battle, and we refer to our weapons. It is a new concept that army is NOT militant! Let this new meaning sink in and show us fresh things about our Father's plan. Please allow the Spirit to be the wonderful counselor and teacher that He is. He is our indwelling Teacher Who leads us into all truth.

So far, we conclude from Scripture that Ya'akov saw dancing angels arranged into two camps or divisions. They had come to rest and rejoice at Machanayim. The angels' message to Ya'akov was not a message of fighting a battle, but to celebrate. We also conclude that Yah's army is a beautifully arrayed and organized body of worshipers. As we lay aside our old model of a combating army, we accept Yah's definition for His army of worshipers.

Part Two

A. Converting: Isaiah 30:32

"Every stroke the LORD lays on them with his punishing rod will be to the music of tambourines and harps, as he fights them in battle with the blows of his arm" (Isaiah 30:32, NIV).

God chose Israel not to be a kingdom of warriors, but a kingdom of priests and kings (Revelation 5:1)!

What are the duties of the priests of the Old Testament? A king rules and a priest ministers to God and to the people.

Now, we think we can decide to conduct spiritual warfare. The reality is that Yah converts our Praise and Worship (P/W will be used for abbreviation for this chapter) into the warfare where and when He needs it – remember He alone is Adonai Tzva'ot, the LORD or Commander of the hosts of heavenly beings. What makes us think we know what is needed? How often are we reminded, "the Battle is the LORD's?!" (1 Samuel 17:47, 2 Chronicles 20:15, Psalms 24:8)

Converting our P/W into warfare is His affair, not ours. How can we tell the Commander where or how to fight? Winning a victory by praising is so opposed to our natural minds. While discussing this with a brother in the LORD, he told me he could see the parallel in the working of a motorcycle engine. He said to me, "The Father converting our P/W into warfare is like the engine taking fuel and air and converting it into power to run the motorcycle." To him, it was very logical.

B. Praisers

If you are a praiser and a dancer, you are in the front of the battle. You are part of Judah (2 Chronicles 20:21). Being one who is in the front of the group, Abba has prepared you to "take" ground! He will often employ you to cut a path that has not been traveled. For example, He may assign you to take the ground for dance in a congregation where there has not been dance before.

1. Garments of Praise

Our battle is NOT with physical giants. Therefore, our warfare is not physical, but rather spiritual (Ephesians 6:12). Our dance clothing is our "fighting uniform." It is likened to the priests dressed for ministry. In comparison, we look at a soldier's uniform adorned with colorful ribbons of decoration and metals of brass.

-48-

A Dream From the Holy Spirit

Our Father can speak to us in dreams. I had a dream, which I had perceived was from God. In my dream I heard these words, "The strength of a man is in what he wears." I saw a military man before he put on his uniform. He was unshaven, dressed in a crumpled tee shirt, and his hair was messed up. He looked neither strong nor like someone we would take orders from! After he put his uniform on, he was transformed! He looked like a different person. His dress has set him apart and given him authority. Notice the elaborate 'dress' of the high priest! The dress of the high priest separates and distinguishes him from all others. He feels different when he is properly dressed. It gives him power, authority and grace. Mercy, humility, and responsibility come with his 'uniform' as well.

How do I feel when I put on my dance garments?

We need not dress in camouflage uniforms and combat boots as I have seen done in prayer meetings or 'spiritual warfare' conferences. NO! We wear the garments of praise (2 Chronicles 20:21).

Bride... exchange your combat boots for dancing shoes!

His ways are higher than ours are. His ways are more pure and refined. Man's ways are crude, rough and militant. Man wants to accomplish things with the brunt of his muscles or with yelling. Have you tried yelling at a child to see how much response you get? This kind of attempt at obtaining victory draws attention to man. But our God demands all the credit. He will not share His glory with any man.

2. Congregational Worship

The enemy hates praise of any kind, whether singing, shouting, raising our hands, etc. For God inhabits the praises of His people.

The enemy hates for the people of Yah to be obedient to His Word, which commands us to praise His Name in the dance (Psalms 149, 150).

An Audience of ONE

Psalm 149 and Psalm 150 are instructions for congregational worship. These instructions are for all the worshipers, not just some. Some will play instruments, some will sing, some will dance. All are instructed to participate. On a certain occasion our dance ministry team was conducting a processional in which we included every person in the building. One of us said, "There is not anyone left to watch." Then we realized He was the One we were doing it for!

[Note: words in brackets are *Strong's* definitions for Hebrew/Greek, respectively.]

"Love the LORD your God with all [whole] your heart [used figuratively for feelings] and with all your soul [breathing creature] and with all your strength [might]" (Deuteronomy 6:5, NIV).

"Teacher, which is the greatest commandment in the Law?" Jesus replied: "'Love the Lord your God with all your heart [thoughts or feelings] and with all your soul [heart, life, mind, soul] and with all your mind [understanding, deep thought]" (Matthew 22:36-37, NIV).

Webster Defines Abandon

1. To give up with the intent of never again claiming one's rights or interests in; to give over or surrender completely.
2. 2.To give (oneself) up without attempt at self-control; a yielding to natural impulses; careless freedom or ease.

By using our whole being, we fulfill our deepest longing to express our love, devotion, adoration, and total abandonment to our God. We can be reckless in our abandonment.

Check Heart Motivation

Why do dancers get more flack than other praisers? For one thing, dancers are visible. Folks don't like visible praisers. It's okay to sit in our seat and raise our hands, and sing; but get out in the aisle, or get in the front and demons will be stirred up!

Misunderstandings in the ministry of dance can lead to jealousy and fear on the part of the congregation and/or the leadership. Since dance is visible and very 'up-front,' it is of up-most importance for the dancer to have a clean and humble heart at ALL times, not just during times of ministry. People will see us dance and they will form their own opinion. It is the Spirit's job to convict, not ours. If our heart is pure before our God, we have nothing to fear from man. If we are dancing in obedience to the Father's commands and the motive of our heart is pure, He is able to take care of everything else.

These scriptures have taught us that as Yah's priests, we do not fight His battles. Our job is to worship Him and praise Him. Aren't you relieved to find out you don't have to become battle weary? Put on your praise garments and let the LORD of the Heavenly Host fight His own battles.

Part Three

A. Restoration of David's Tabernacle

Were you aware King David established twenty-four hour, seven days a week, worship in music and song? One third of the Levites were assigned for this important task. He had musicians and singers on duty around the clock for worship and praise. Let's stop here and picture this in our minds. Why did Yahweh want twenty-four hour music in song? Who is in the tabernacle in the middle of the night?

"Praise the LORD, all you servants of the LORD who minister by night in the house of the LORD. Lift up your hands in the sanctuary and praise the LORD. May the LORD, the Maker of heaven and earth, bless you from Zion" (Psalms 134:1-3, NIV).

"Those who were musicians, heads of Levite families, stayed in the rooms of the temple and were exempt from other duties because they were responsible {on duty for singing AMP} for the work {of singing} day and night" (1 Chronicles 9:33, NIV).

"These are the men David put in charge of the music in the house of the LORD after the ark came to rest there. They ministered with music before the tabernacle, the Tent of Meeting, until Solomon built the temple of the LORD in Jerusalem. They performed their duties according to the regulations laid down for them"(1 Chronicles 6:31-32, NIV).

Abba's Word leaves us no doubts! Joyful, qualified singers accompanied with loud music played skillfully on varied instruments are what please Him (1 Chronicles 6, 1 Chronicles 15,16, 2 Chronicles 29:25).

Don't let anyone tell you Praise and Worship is entertainment or mere emotionalism! Sure, some may not have a purely motivated heart when they worship. We must remember there are those who are young in the LORD, who will dance, sing or jump because of their great love for the Father. Also, our enemy will always attempt to counterfeit the genuine worship. Some may look humble. They may sing or use sign language in a way that may minister, but only Abba knows their heart. We have not been selected to judge the person's heart. Don't go there, lest we end up like David's wife, Michal, causing our lives to become fruitless for God (2 Samuel 6:16-23). If you are told you are entertaining, respond like one of the dancers in our ministry, "That's right, I'm entertaining my Father!"

B. Tent of Meeting for Today

"Do you not know that your body is a temple of the Holy Spirit, who is in you, whom you have received from God? You are not your own; you were bought at a price. Therefore honor God with your body" (1 Corinthians, NIV).

Notice He said 'your body,' not your spirit. Our body is extremely important to Him. It is holy. One could go so far as to say our body is spiritual since it is a spiritual house for Spirit God. Our body is the Tent of Meeting today. The primary service inside the Tent of Meeting today is for offering sacrifices, the same as it was when Moshe/Moses built the Tabernacle.

"Therefore, I urge you, brothers, in view of God's mercy, to offer your bodies as living sacrifices, holy and pleasing to God-- this is your spiritual act of worship" (Romans 12:1, NIV).

Since each believer is the temple of God, we are continually offering ourselves as a living sacrifice. We should give the fruit of our lips in praise (Hebrews 13:15), pray without ceasing (1 Thessalonians 5:17), and live a humble and compassionate life (1 Peter 3:9), knowing we are in His Presence twenty-four hour a day. Perhaps this is why God put it in David's heart to institute twenty-four hour praise and worship in the tabernacle and later in the Temple Solomon built. The continuous praise and worship in the tabernacle and later in the Temple was merely a type and shadow of the 'temple not made with human hands,' which we are.

Finale

In this chapter, the Ruach/Spirit has changed our understanding of 'army' to line up with His. We have used the plumb-line of His Word to set us straight. Now we understand as we live a life of worship, the Commander of the Heavenly Host converts our worship of/to Him into "blows to His enemy." This is exciting, good news to us, the Kingdom of priests! We are thrilled and relieved to find out we are not required to conduct spiritual warfare. Our jobs are simple: worship Him with our whole body, strength and heart.

We invite you to enter the dance and experience the joy of the LORD. Let Him enjoy your sacrifice of worship. Allow Him to use you as a model to lead others into the expression of offering their whole body in praise. Blessings will overtake you as the LORD of the dance leads you into this satisfying expression of worship. You will be amazed, as the LORD of Host converts your offering unto Him into His mighty blows to render His enemy non-effective.

An example for converting praise and worship into victory...

Keys to Spiritual Battle

2 Chronicles 20:12:

- ♦ vs 3: fast
- ♦ vs 4: yearn for Him with all your desire
- ♦ vs 12: pray ... we do not know what to do; prayer gets His plan
- ♦ vs 15: remember that the battle is not your own
- ♦ vs 18: worship
- ♦ vs 19: some stood to praise w/ VERY loud voice
- ♦ vs 21: send out the praisers FIRST in their praise garments
- ♦ vs 22: Praise and worship sets into motion the victory of the LORD.

Because of the great victory, the fear of the LORD came upon all kingdoms that heard the LORD had fought Israel's enemies! This is the spiritual warfare plan for today's battles. Are we using it?

6

North and South Dance Teams

A ngelic Dancers of Old Foretell Israel's Future.

As we discovered in our last chapter, Genesis thirty-two tells us about when Ya'akov/Jacob saw the angels of God that met him. Ya'akov named that place Machanayim (meaning two camps, CJB). What did Ya'akov see? He saw two camps of rejoicing, dancing angels. In this chapter we shall discover how this prophetic scene speaks volumes about Ya'akov's family, both at that present time and well into the future.

On his way home to his father's house that night (Genesis 31:30), Ya'akov became afraid of his brother Esav/Esau, who, he assumed, was coming to kill him. Considering he saw the two encampments of celebrating angels (messengers of God), he obeyed the vision and divided his family, flocks, cattle and camels into TWO CAMPS. In chapter thirty-two verse eleven he prays, "I crossed over the Jordan with only my staff. But now I have become TWO CAMPS."

Hundreds of years before the house (kingdom, or camp) of Israel gets split into TWO, our Father shows Ya'akov what is to come by pulling back the veil to expose future scenes. In obedience to this revelation, Ya'akov divides, or splits, his family and possessions into two groups. We shall discover these two divisions of angelic dancers are a type and shadow of the two houses of Israel dancing to the House of God.

In this very place Ya'akov encounters the famous wrestling match with the pre-incarnate God-Man, wins, gets his identity changed (hence, a name change), and names the place P'ni El [face of God] (Genesis 32:31).

Bethel With Many Names

Have you noticed that places, people, and events in the Bible have more than one name? This can be challenging to keep up, so let's trace some names. Ya'akov's grandfather, Avraham/Abraham, built his second altar at this place, which he named, Beit-El (Bethel), or House of God (Genesis 12:8).

In Genesis twenty-eight, as Ya'akov leaves his father Yitz'chak/Isaac, he receives his dream from God in this same place, Beit-El. Here he builds an altar, sets a stone for a monument and anoints it to consecrate it to God (verse 18). Some thirty years later, Ya'akov returns to this place (Beit-El), and he names it "two camps" and P'ni El.

There is one more treasure we must unearth before we get to the bottom line. The oriental expression, 'to cover his face,' means one is hiding his sin. In Genesis 32:20, Ya'akov said "I will appease him with the present that goeth before me, and afterward I will see his face"(KJV). We can conclude from this expression, that to see someone "face to face" would indicate that there was nothing hidden between the two, especially sin. It is in this place that Ya'akov wrestles with Yah and wins, where there are two camps of dancing angels, and where he renames that place P'ni El, (face of God). He met with God face to face and did not die! In Exodus 33:20 God tells Moshe/Moses that no one may see Him and live. There was nothing hidden between Ya'akov and God.

The Place of Rest

The prophetic picture of the house of God (Bethel) shows us that the Father's children will be two camps (Machanayim) rejoicing and celebrating with the Mighty Yah, face to face (P'ni-El.) Or to say it another way, when we see the two camps of Israel dancing in a place of rest (remember Machanayim means rest in a tent), His children WILL see the face of God!

This place is not a place for battles and warfare but for rejoicing and celebrating. The two camps will come to rest in a place of merriment and shalom. This is the very place Ya'akov receives his name change. Could it be in this place that we, the presently split house of Israel, receive our new name, becoming ECHAD in the hand of the Father (Ezekiel 37:19)? Could this be the place we become the 'one new man' spoken of in Ephesians 2:13-16?

Ya'akov had become a new man. He had worked twenty years for his possessions. He was wealthy. He was freed from one master, his father-in-law Lavan, to become a bond-slave to Another. God had put His 'mark' on Ya'akov by striking his hip socket. This was, so to speak, the 'piercing of the ear,' as the master taking the awl to the slave's ear when that freed slave chose to remain under the care of the master for life (Deuteronomy 15:17, Exodus 21:6).

Picture Worth a Thousand Words

Each one of Israel's sons was born to mothers who were idol worshipers. This shows us that all of Israel is rooted in idolatry. Imagine for a moment each of the four mothers of Israel raising her sons. How much idolatry did each receive in his up bringing? How much idolatry was woven into the separate personalities? We need to ponder this to come to the reality that ALL of Israel was prone to pagan practices. As both camps discover their roots, both camps will repent and come to Machanayim, the place of rest and rejoicing.

This prophetic picture tells us many things, some of which Abba will yet unfold. Each house of Israel will come to grips with its idolatrous past, repent, to then join their brothers in celebration. The camps of dancing angels show us the emphasis on praise and worship as both houses come together to worship our Father in the "congregation of the First Born."

"But you have come to Mount Zion, to the heavenly Jerusalem, the city of the living God. You have come to thousands upon thousands of angels in joyful assembly, to the church of the firstborn, whose names are written in heaven. You have come to God, the judge of all men, to the spirits of righteous men made perfect ..." (Hebrews 12:22-23, NIV).

The emphasis is on praise and worship! The angels were not writing commentaries or debating scriptures. The angels were not even studying scripture. The angels were dancing. Why were they dancing? As we found out in chapter two, dance is the Biblical definition for joy. Dance is joy expressed with our whole body. Even angels dance to express joy. As the passage in Hebrews records for our understanding, we all will join in a joyful assembly. How else will we join the dancing angels except by dancing?

Finale

Ya'akov was on his journey to his father's house. Both houses of Israel are on our way home to our Father's House. The two camps of angelic dancers portray the two houses of Israel, Judah and Ephraim. The dancing angels come to the place of rest, Machanayim. Both houses of Israel come to the place of rest. Remember that all are on our way home to Abba's house. This place of rest for the two houses is where we all can come to worship our Father together.

The rejoicing takes place before we get there. For sure we will meet Abba face to face, since Ya'akov our ancestor did see Yah face to face in 'that place' of rest. We are able to meet with Him Face to Face, with nothing hindering our relationship because of the Perfect Sacrifice of the Lamb of Yah, Our Yahshua/Jesus. There is no sin hindering our relationship.

In the prophetic picture of these two camps of dancing angels we see the house from the north, Ephraim, and we see the house of the south, Judah. In other words, we see the dancers of the north and the dancers of the south coming together in the place of rest to worship and celebrate. As these two dance teams (or houses) come together we each will retain some characteristics of our personalities. We each will bring delightful flavors and spices to the banquet table. Here is where the two dance teams become blended into one organized worshiping 'army.' Or this is where we become one pleasingly fragrant offering. Just as Ya'akov received a new name in the place of Bethel, so too, the North and South dance teams will receive a new name.

We clearly see this worship experience of the two camps of dancing angels at Bethel occurs before we arrive at the Father's House. We can say the Father's House is the Holy of Holies, for this is His throne. The 'two camp worship experience' takes place in the Holy Place, or the Inner Court. In the Holy Place we find one of articles of furniture being the table of Shewbread, or the Bread of His Presence or Bread of His Face (the translation of P'ni El). What an amazing parallel! The remaining furniture items are the altar of incense, representing the prayers of the saints and the never-ending light coming from the menorah/lampstand. Each of these pieces of furniture indicates a twenty-four hour worship experience. However, not one of these articles could continue in its function without the service of a priest. A priest was needed to replenish the oil for the continual burning of the menorah. A priest was needed to bake the Shewbread and deliver it fresh each week to the table. Lastly, a priest was needed to keep the fire burning on the altar of incense.

Let these articles of furniture teach us a very important lesson; we have a desperate need for fresh oil, fresh fire, and fresh bread on a daily basis in order to worship our LORD, or serve in the Holy Place. It is in this place, the Holy Place, where Judah and Ephraim will serve together in worship to our Father on the way to His house. Or, putting it another way, both houses of Israel will worship together in the Holy Place on our way to the Holy of Holies.

North and South Dance Teams

7

Dancing on the Hills of Ephraim

A "day will come when the watchman on Mount Ephraim will call, 'Come, lets go up to Tziyon (Zion) to Adonai our God'" (Jeremiah 31:5, CJB).

Growing up in the 1980's my parents had me go to church every Sunday. Week after week, year after year, I went to Sunday school and church. I learned about dynamic biblical characters such as Adam and Eve, Noah and his ark, and King David. With the stories always came a lesson about life and how to live it. Each story, which was placed in my soul, would eventually build a bridge that would connect me to who I am today. As I begin to mature in my walk with Yah I wanted to dig deeper into the scripture and challenge my traditional views. With a challenging and an open mind I was led to the surprising knowledge that Israel had two houses. With this new (to me) knowledge I re-read every scripture verse that spoke of Israel, Judah and Ephraim. This search led me to the above verse in Jeremiah 31. I had read Jeremiah 31 a dozen times and it meant nothing to me.

Now, after discovering my heritage as an Ephraimite, I wonder who are the watchman on Mount Ephraim which is spoken of in Jeremiah 31:5. Have you ever wondered about these watchmen?

If you have, this chapter is for you. "Dancing on the Hills of Ephraim" will take us on a journey that will ultimately change the way we look at ourselves as believers in the Messiah. Through this chapter we will see how Abba romances all of Israel from every nation to be one with Him in dance.

Who are we to have the desire to dance before the Creator of the universe?

The Ingathering of Yah's Children

"Why do I have the desire to dance before the God of Israel?" Have you ever asked yourself this question? If you have you are not alone. I have asked this question to myself numerous times. As discussed in previous chapters, we all have within us a divine longing to return to the One Who created us. Yah is our creator. He is gathering His children from all over the world, back to His kingdom, the commonwealth of Israel. The answer to my question I found in Jeremiah 31.

"I love you with an everlasting love; this is why in my grace I draw you to Me. Once again, I will build you; you will be rebuilt, virgin of Israel. Once again, equipped with your tambourines, you will go out and dance with the merrymakers. Once again, you will plant vineyards on the hills of Shomron (Samaria), and those doing the planting will have use of its fruits" (Jeremiah 31:2-4, CJB).

"For this is the covenant I will make with the house of Israel, after those days," says Adonai: "I will put my Torah (law) within them and write it on their hearts" (Jeremiah 31:32, CJB).

Abba is summoning Israel with a romantic love. Through His love, He is drawing Israelites from across the world to Himself. Our Father proclaims His love for us in Jeremiah 31:2. With no mistake He makes it clear He is drawing us to Himself. Jeremiah's prophetic word, reveal to us who we are, and what Yah has laid out for our future. The Almighty Yah deeply yearns for Ephraim's return (Jeremiah 31:19). Abba speaks to us with such a passion showing His deep love and affection He has for us. Can we hear the passion in His voice when He speaks to us? "I LOVE YOU WITH AN EVERLASTING LOVE." Our Father is the only entity in the entire universe Who can wrap us in His love. His love is so powerful, that His own voice romances us to be by His side. One reason why He is gathering us (His children) is that we can dance and worship Him. He is the Almighty Spirit God and desires our worship through dance.

With His love as our security we do not have to rely on man for our needs, but look to the Father for every need. When Abba calls, He is asking us to be His. He is the one Who will ultimately take care of us. Who else can offer this all-consuming love? We need to seek a direct intercourse (connection) and union with the Father so we can merge and be ONE with Him. Once we are one with Him, His strength will be our strength.

"Finally, grow powerful in union with the Lord, in union with His mighty strength" (Ephesians 6:10, CJB).

He is gathering back His children from the nations from which He sent them; to dance on the Hills of Ephraim.

Hearing the Call

Have you heard the call from the Father? If you have, you will know He is calling you to be His Bride. But the Father wants His people to repent and then He will usher them in for their return trip. Repenting is the most important step in establishing a relationship with/to the Father. The act of repentance is one of the biggest hurdles that stand in our way of returning. Will we listen to the call from our Husband and arise to take our place as His Bride (Isaiah 54:5)? Jeremiah 6:17 teaches that Abba has set watchmen over the people to proclaim His holy calling. The people did not listen to the watchman, will we?

Will we go forth to dance before His majestic throne? The Father will call a multitude of people to the dance, but if they are disobedient, they will miss out on the blessing. Every individual the Father has created with "the handiwork of an artist (Song of Songs 7:2)" has the desire to dance. If we truly love the Father as "He first loved us," we want to experience Him in every way. The Prophet Jeremiah prophesied we are being called to the dance. As declared in chapter one, ("Entering into the Presence") our Father has already done His part, now it's our turn.

Understanding the Call

We as Believers in Yahshua/Jesus must understand who we are. Knowing who we are and where we are going is vital to our relationship with the God of Israel. Once we realized our soul/spirit is the Part that connects us with Yah, we can never be defeated. If we know who we are in God, then His knowledge of good and purity will be instilled in us. The Father protects His children, and when we depend only on Him, He will defeat our enemies (See chapter "DANCING WARRIOR" for further detail on spiritual warfare through dance).

By understanding the call of Abba, the reality of "Who is Israel" will become clearer. We are Israel! Could this be the very reason why so many non-Jewish brothers and sisters are drawn to Israel? To find the answers we will review Romans 2:14-15 and Jeremiah 31:32. To find the first key; we must understand who we are. We catch a glimpse of our identity in Romans 2:14-15.

"For whenever Gentiles, who have no Torah (Law), do naturally what Torah requires, then these, even though they don't have Torah, for themselves are Torah! For their lives show that the conduct the Torah dictates is written in their hearts" (Romans 2:14-15, CJB).

Torah was given to the children of Israel. Torah is Israel, Israel is Torah, and if the Gentiles of Romans two are Torah then they are

Israel as well. "Written in their hearts," does this look familiar? Our second key is found in Jeremiah 31:32 where Yah said He would write Torah within the heart of Israel. Paul declares in Romans 2:14-15 that Gentiles are Torah, for it is written in their hearts. Now we have unlocked the treasure of, "knowing who we are." We are Israel and will dance to restore the whole House of Israel. The time to arise in the dance is now!

Come Forth Watchmen

"The watchman of Ephraim is with my God..."(Hosea 9:8, CJB).

Who is our Father calling as He is gathering His children? He is calling those who have an ear to hear. These are people who want to worship the Father in spirit and in truth (John 4:23). To see an indication, of which the Father is calling, we will look at the word watchmen.

Jeremiah 31:5

"For a day will come when the watchman on Mount Ephraim will call, 'Come, lets go up to Tziyon (Zion) to Adonai our God'" (Jeremiah 31:5, CJB).

Notzrim is the present day term in Israel for Christian. Notzrim is derived from Strong's #H5341. Natsar is the primitive root meaning: to guard in a good sense, to protect and maintain, observe, preserve and watcher. Natsar is the Hebrew word that is used for watchmen. If we were to replace watchmen with Christian then this verse would read:

"For a day will come when the watchman/ Christian on Mount Ephraim will call, 'Come, lets go up to Tziyon (Zion) to Adonai our God'" (Jeremiah 31:5, CJB).

Psalms 25:10

Psalms 25:10 also uses the word natsar. "All the paths of Yahweh are mercy and truth to the keepers of His covenant and it's testimonies." (Literal Bible with *Strong's* #'s)

The same natsar #H5341, is used in Psalm 25:10. The word keeper is used in this verse. Once again we will replace natsar with Christian and the verse will read:

"All the paths of Yahweh are mercy and truth to the Christians/watchman of His covenant and it's testimonies."

The Father is yearning for His Notrzim/Christians return.

Ephraim's Flight

As Ephraim and Yah's "notrzim" we have a role to play in the game of dance. But what is our job as Yahweh's watchmen? The prophet Habakkuk further explains our role as Ephraim as watchmen.

"I will stand at my watchpost; I will station myself on the rampart. I will look to see what (God) will say through me and what I will answer when I am reproved" (Habakkuk 2:1, CJB).

"I will stand upon my watch, and set me upon the tower, and will watch to see what He will say unto me, and what I shall answer when I am reproved" (Habakkuk 2:1, KJV).

We learn from Habakkuk that watchmen are to stay still before the Lord where He has positioned them. With humbleness, the watchmen look for the Spirit of Yah to speak to them. Yet, when Yah rebukes them they do honor His word. In both translations Complete Jewish Bible and King James Version the word "reproved" has been used. Reproved means to charge with a fault orally; to chide; to rebuke. Watchmen are very cautious people. They listen to the Father before they speak from Him. They wait on the Lord to move from within them. Then they will react accordingly.

Abba has called us His watchman. Will we step into our role as watchmen? By being His watchmen there is several other duties, which we must uphold. We must watch, protect, maintain order, and preserve His laws. As His watchmen we have a job to preserve the Holy Dance. How do we preserve? We will preserve the dance where it is meant to be, in His congregations of worship.

Ephraim and Judah are being re-united and restored. With this reunion, we see a revival of Christians and Jews coming to the knowledge of dance through worship. Through this knowledge of dance, liberty and freedom will soon enter into congregations of worship. As the "arts" re-enter our worship times we must question why and Who we are worshiping.

Satan and His Perversions

The arts of worship and praise (which are used to exalt our God) were created by our Father to glorify Himself. However, for the most part, Satan has stolen these arts from the Father's congregations of worship. For millennium, the enemy has perverted and prostituted all the arts. Satan's scheme went so far as to twist the holy dance originally used to worship our King, and to change it to instead be used for the worship of the human flesh—or even Satan himself. From the beginning our enemy's plan has been to rob our Father of His rightful worship. Let us see what Satan has done to the dance.

Satan has taken our offering of praise and worship to defile it, because he wants to have glory in the dance. Satan manipulates what the Father has established and uses it for his own foul deeds. Satan knows we all have within us the call to dance before our Creator. If we allow him, he will use the calling against us for his own use. Knowing Satan wants to destroy us, it is important to put on the whole armor of God (Ephesians 6:13-17). By placing His armor around us He will protect our mind and body.

We hear of people dancing and singing in clubs every night. Young men and women are dancing in bars as strippers. This kind of dance is constantly being glorified by the radio and television. Our children are seeing and hearing Satan's deeds every day. Yet what do we do about it? Are we choosing to hear what Satan has done, or what the Father has done? Every time we allow our worship to be used in a worldly way, our temple is further destroyed. Our temple can only withstand so much, till it will self-destruct. Our mind and body need to be safeguarded against worldly actions. When we join the world in its perverted acts, Satan revels in delight over our mistake!

Dance of the Molten Calf

Exodus 32:19-20, shows us how Satan perverted the dance. What did Moshe/Moses see as he approached the camp, and where were the people stationed? He saw the Israelites stationed in a circle dancing around the molten god. The thought of something being worship besides Yahweh anger him. What did he do? He ground the calf into powder and made the people drink it! Further more, for this blasphemous act, he ordered the Levites to kill their brothers for their sin. Three thousand men were slain on that day. Wow, what a punishment for worshiping and dancing to a false god. Have we ever used dance as an unholy act?

What does the dance of the molten calf teach us? We find dance has been used as an unholy act for thousands of years. Whether it was for communing with a false deity or using it for personal gain, their dance was not holy in His sight. We see Satan likes to be praised through the dance. To whom are we commanded to dance? Abba or Satan? If our dance is not for the Father then our praise is being offered to Satan. The tragedy is that Abba is stripped from His rightful worship.

Every time we move in the dance something is being worship. Our body moves with the motion and the rhythm of the music. When we move our body to the music, what are we praising? We should be praising Abba Father. If not, we put ourselves at danger for the enemy to come into our lives. Some people may look at this theory and may think we are taking this to the extreme. But it is so logical, dance unto the Father, or Satan? We cannot worship both. The dance of the molten calf teaches us that we can only praise one God through the dance. Look what happened to the Israelites as they danced their heart and soul around and around the molten calf. We can look to this passage in scripture to be a format on how we should dance unto the Father.

Dance Unto the Father

It is important to understand what dance is and what it can accomplish. If we see the power of dance in worship, then we will realize bondage can be broken and strongholds will cave in. Through our dance of victory, Satan's plan against Yah's people will collapse! Dance can express the innermost desires of our heart. When we, as His children, learn how to invoke the Ruach/ Holy Spirit, and dance in the atmosphere of praise and worship, situations around us will change.

In the past eight years that I have been dancing, there have been numerous of miracles that I have seen through the dance. People would come to me weary and broken hearted, not knowing what to do in their life. As I taught them worship through dance and they begin to grow in their worship to the Father their weary and broken heart begin to heal. Yah filled the void that was placed there with His love.

Dancing unto Abba is in our soul; He desires it. Just by tapping into our soul, to pull out our worship to Him, we will begin to feel the release of dance. By moving our feet, our body will start to move with the music and we will praise the Father.

At the same time, we must summon the Ruach, which will only heighten our praise to the Father. I find that one of the best times to seek Him is when I am sick or depressed. Every time when I have a cold or flu, I dance. Although people tell me that I need to stay in bed and calm down, dancing while I am sick makes me feel better. Even though I have become weak in my flesh, I still can worship the Father and ask for His forgiveness and healing power. After my worship I feel my symptoms ease, and my chest feels lighter. We can use dance as worship in every situation in our life. There is healing and restoration in the dance; the Father wants us to use this form of worship.

We are in control of our own actions, of how we dance to the Father. Everything we do will demonstrate how we love the Father. There are only two thoughts that we should think as we prepare ourselves to dance; will we choice the "dance of life" or the "dance of death"? If we choose life then He will bless us.

"I call on heaven and earth to witness against you today that I have presented you with life and death, the blessing and the curse. Therefore, choose life, so that you will live you and your descendants" (Deuteronomy 30:19, CJB).

1. Using Miryam/Miriam as an example, will I dance as Miryam danced, and proclaim that He is highly exulted?

OR

2. Will I dance as the children of Israel danced, around the molten calf?

Our Father is looking for dancers to lead the way to the full restoration of Israel. The call has been sent out, we have a choice to accept or decline. Dance as worship is returning, as Ephraim is reuniting with Judah! We have to thank Judah for preserving Hebraic dance as a form of worship. The Jews (Judah) have kept dance as worship, through good and bad times. Even through their exile, they returned still dancing. (Judah was exiled to Babylon 586 B.C. Return of the exiles to Jerusalem took place around 536 B.C.) If Judah did not keep dance alive, then "dance as worship" could have been lost, perhaps forever. Ephraim arise and take your place. Judah help Ephraim take back what is his!

Before we advance in our progression to the Holy of Holies, let us imagine we are in ancient Israel. Imagine we are all dressed in white, dancing on the Hills of Ephraim. As we dance we are at the edge overlooking the valley, which is beneath. The power of the mountain is an indication that as we dance on the Hills we are dancing in the palm of our Father's hand. Imagine this prophetic picture as we dance and worship Abba.

We can conclude from this chapter the following:

♦   Yah is calling His people with a romantic love
♦   He has called us to be Israel
♦   We are called to be His watchmen

All Israel Dances Toward The Tabernacle

Dancing On the Hills of Ephraim

8

A Challenge For Both Ephraim and Judah

Worshiping the Father through dance can be one of the most exciting adventures that we get to do in our lifetime. We don't have to dance for our Father we GET to. We know He desires our worship. However, as we worship the Father, we need to show respect to all of His creation. This respect includes showing honor and approval toward one another. Could this be a challenge for us? Can both houses/families of Israel worship differently but still remain in unity? Worshiping differently but in unity will be a challenge for us all. But through the love of Yahshua/Jesus even this is possible.

Individual Identities

There is no doubt, the rhythm and movement of dance is powerful. With every action there is a reaction. This law holds true in our worship as well. Our worship is the action. Our Father makes the reaction take place. We worship Abba, and in turn He uses it where it is needed [See chapter on DANCING WARRIOR]. We can vaguely comprehend what goes on in the spiritual world as our praise and worship ascends toward the heavens. We may think we know what is happening but in reality we are only making guesses, which will satisfy our own mind. Our actions can be pure and clean before the Father, or we can worship for self-gain. We can further gain pleasure through our worship to and with the Father by experiencing Him in every way.

As we know, Israel has two houses each with their own individual identity. Both houses will present different types of worship styles to Abba. Ephraim has their style of worship, as does Judah. Practicing Jews and practicing Christians both worship the Father in their unique fashion. The Jews pour out their worship from their heart to the Father as they wait for their Messiah. By acknowledging the feasts of Israel, they are somewhat content in their worship. While worshiping the true Messiah Yahshua/Jesus, the Christians await for His return.

Is it wrong for Christians and Jews to worship differently? The Father wants worship that comes from the pure in heart. Yah has given us individuality and we should not be ashamed of it. Would you want your worship dance to be a cookie cut out of another's cookie dough? Or would you want it to be your own individual creation that you have developed only for and to the Father?

When the Father brings people into our lives to show us a different form of worship, we should respond with acceptance and gratitude that we have yet another way to praise Him. Let Israel praise the Almighty Yah; our praise and worship will be restricted no more! Without question, Abba desires dance from both houses of Israel. He has not chosen Judah over Ephraim or vice versa. If my dance is acceptable to the Father then it should be acceptable to other people as well. Remember we all want what our Father wants. Right? If we exclude another brother's worship from our congregation and force him to conform to our methods we will become a type of Pharaoh putting Israel back into bondage. How could we ever get out of that one? I would not want to be the one to explain to God why I held His people in bondage. Let us discuss more types of worship and praise dance acceptable to the Father beyond the circle worship.

Halal Praise

In recent years I have heard questions concerning the proper form of worship dance to the Father. In this ongoing debate we have Christians say only spirit led dance is allowed. On the other hand Jews say only circle dance is permitted. Who is right? Why is this even a big concern? Yah wants worship from every nation on Earth. If we don't praise Him the rocks will! Would you want a rock to take your place in praising Abba?

So let us boast about our Creator through our praise. Don't let anyone tell you your dance is too showy. I have been told that my dance is too showy since when I dance, it comes from my soul. When I present my worship to the Father, His light shines through me to the people. Abba is the only One who brings out the best in my worship to Him. He draws my worship from within. Music stimulates me to worship the Father; in fact it brings me new joy every time I worship Him. I will boast about my God and will present the best worship I can to Him. *Strong's* #H1984 halal (haw-lal) is the Hebrew word for praise. It means to shine, make a show, to boast and thus to be clamorously foolish, to rave, to celebrate, glory and give light colorful, sounds.

"I will praise Adonai as long as I live" and "praise Him from my soul" (Psalm 146:1-2 CJB). Our praise and worship will come from our soul. And when it does Yah wants us to make a show with His light shining through and we will boast about what He has done. Are we making halal praise about the God of Israel?

David's praise is coming from deep within his soul (which is his heart). He is expressing his feelings about His God and interpreting them through praise and dance. Our halal praise word also can be associated with movement or dance. We could say halal praise means we are making a "presentational praise dance," in celebration, and thus are shining forth with His awesome glory. First we will minister to the Father and second to the people, shining His glory and boasting about our God. All "servants of Adonai will give praise" (Psalms 113:1) and boast about the God of Israel. Again, the Hebrew word that is used here is halal. Abba is commanding His people to boast about Him. Are we obeying? Are we boasting?

Ancient Halal

King David's Psalm to the Lord makes it clear that he used halal praise. He cried out with a passion, "I will give thanks in the great assembly, I will give you praise among huge crowds of people (Psalm 35:18). We see David praising God by making a show among the great assembly of people. Can you make a 'show' quietly?

Let us travel back in time to ancient Israel. As we enter into the courtyard of the Temple in Jerusalem we see crowds of people surrounding a presentation (or 'show') that is taking place. Right before our eyes we see King David dancing and shouting praises to the God of Israel. Usually the kings are not the ones who put on the shows it is the court jester. But David dances to the beat of a different drum. He is putting on a show about the Creator of the universe. The One from whom he received the Breath of life is the same Breath, Who now dwells in us.

King David is not only ministering to the Father but he is also being the light that will shine and set him and Israel apart from the nations. Or as a dear sister told me, this type of praise is a sound and light show!! A sound and light show is what is being brought forth or birthed as we dance and praise the Father. Light and sound transcending through the heavens, proclaiming the one true God, the God of Israel. What a show!

Judah will tell Ephraim that his presentational and spontaneous dances are not what God desires. However Ephraim will tell Judah that organized and choreographed dance is not scriptural and is emotionalism and fleshy. Consequently we have conflicting views from both branches of Israel's olive tree. To what extend will Yahshua go to bring both families/houses together?

Abba honors those who will take time to worship Him in a rehearsed manner. Rehearsed worship ministers to the Father and to the people. He honors this because time is taken to practice, to meditate and to have self-discipline in the body. But when the "Spirit" starts to move and you are encouraged to worship through dance prophetically, let nothing stand in your way and let Him move your feet as you worship. However He honors only those worshiping from a pure heart. If you find yourself in a situation that will cause people to bring judgment upon your worship, refer them to halal praise and go on about the Father's business!!

There are different forms of praise from both "families" of Ya'akov/Jacob, but equal weights and measures on both sides must be honored. Adonai detests "false weights and false measures" (Proverbs 20:10). The house of Israel and the house of Judah do not want to be a stench in His nostrils. Instead of griping and complaining about the different forms of praise to the Father, let us experience Him in every way He has to offer. What is so wrong with that?

Yadah Praise

Let us see the authority carried by the intense worship of the Almighty's "praise army." Every deviled vessel will bow down to the Almighty. The 2nd Chronicles 20:21 records the account of the people who go out as His "praise army." Let's do a word study to see what is taking place as the praise army went out.

"After consulting with the people, he appointed those who would sing to Adonai and praise the splendor of His holiness as they went out ahead of the army, saying 'Give thanks to Adonai, for his grace continues forever.' Then during the time when they were singing and praising, Adonai brought the surprise attack against the people of Amon, Mo'av, and Mount Se'ir who had come to fight Y'hudah; and they were defeated" (2nd Chronicles 20: 21-22, CJB).

First we see that singers were appointed by an authority figure. Next we see the line "praise and splendor." Again the Hebrew word that is used here is halal. The "praise army" went ahead of the combat army making a show about their God of Israel and boasting about His mighty power. As they approached their enemy they chanted, "Give thanks to Adonai, for His grace continues forever." The Hebrew word that is used in the above passage for thanks is yadah (yaw-daw) *Strong's* #H3034. Yadah means the hand, to throw (a stone, an arrow) to revere or worship (with extended hands) confess and praise.

Imagine these people shouting and jumping with extended hands giving thanks to their God. Their yadah praise made these people into a quiver and their praise became the arrow that brought down the enemy. Look what happens when these people were praising Adonai, and look Who defeated their enemies. Yah did not tell the people to go fight with their brut force first. It was commanded to praise Adonai, so that He would fight for them. Who are we, to fight Adonai Tzva'ot battles? We are mortal men placed on the earth to praise nothing else but Adonai Tzva'ot.

When it came to worshiping the Father king David had it down pat. He states that he calls on Adonai "who is worthy of praise; and I am saved from my enemies" (Psalms 18:1, CJB). Who did David call on and what happen when He was called upon? You see David knew the awesome power of the Creator, and what happens when He praises Him.

This makes my life a lot easier; all Abba wants me to do is praise Him and He in-turn will defeat my enemies. What great news! Yah goes into battle before we do, He wants to protect His bride. Just as a husband will protect his wife and children from danger, in-turn Yah will also protect His bride and children. Adonai is our strength and shield. When we open our heart to Him, He will help us, so we can be filled with joy to praise our King (Psalms 28:7).

We can conclude that Yah desires our yadah and halal praise. And when we praise Him, He will fight for us! Just think of the tremendous possibilities if Jews and Christians would only start to praise Abba. That sounds and looks like a restoration to me!

The Power of Love

Loving one another as Yahshua loves us will prove to be a success, as Yah restores Israel. When Ephraim uses the love that Yahshua gave, Ephraim will no longer be jealous of Judah. With this same love Judah will come to know their Messiah Yahshua and Judah will no longer provoke Ephraim. "Ephraim's jealousy will cease, those who harass Judah will be cut off. Ephraim will stop envying Judah, and Judah will stop provoking Ephraim" (Isaiah 11:13, CJB). In order to obtain the full restoration of all Israel, equal weights and measures must be used in both houses regarding our worship sacrifice. In the end both houses/families will realize that they must worship in unity and harmony, and give Yah first place before themselves. Remember it is important to show love and compassion to our brother. Both houses will bring their worship dance onto the "worship floor" and together they will praise the God of Israel with love and compassion.

"How good and pleasant it is when brothers live together in unity" (Psalms 133:1, NIV).Loving those who have not found Yahshua will aid them in their salvation with Him. Imagine Ephraim loving Judah even though he has not heard the message of salvation. Or imagine Judah loving Ephraim by teaching him the feasts of the LORD and the ways of Torah.

By Ephraim's love for Judah, Yahshua will be shown to them as the Messiah Who comes from the root of Jesse. Judah's love for Ephraim will open their eyes to Torah, which will open the eyes of

Judah to the reality that Yahshua has become the living Torah. With these steps toward restoration we will begin to see the power of dance worship to the Father.

The Power of Dance

When Yah calls you into His ministry of dance, be prepared to be on the front line of battle (2nd Chronicles 20:21-22). We all can worship the Father through dance whether it is in our home or congregation. But when we step into the roll of ministering to the people, this puts us into a different category. Each of us walks in different anointings and this situation follows true. The anointing on the dance allows Abba to destroy bondages while strongholds collapse. This is the power of dance in worship. We are, in essence, setting people free. We become a type of Moshe/Moses as he led the Israelites out of Egypt. Moshe led the people out of bondage from Pharaoh. What happened when Moshe freed the slaves? Pharaoh came after Moshe. This will be true with us as well, as we lead people out of and make them bond slaves to each other.

Satan will come after those who are creating havoc in his playground. Be prepared for Satan to attack from all ends of the spectrum. He can use family, friends, and even congregational members. But be of good cheer! Remember what happened to Pharaoh in the end. When Pharaoh tried to kill Moshe, Pharaoh was thrown into the sea. This will be true in the case of Satan coming after the people of Yah. Yah will defeat our enemies for us and spew them into a sea. We have it easy. All we have to do is praise Him, and love the ones who spitefully use us.

Remembering Egypt

Looking back on the past eight years of my life, when I write about the power of dance, and how Satan will come after you, I speak from experience. A while back, Yah brought me to a certain congregation to learn about my Hebraic roots in Him. A few months later, I experienced Abba in a new form; I was dancing for Him.

It happened quickly, one night after a Passover Seder I was walking with this girl who was one of the dancers. I explained how I enjoyed her and her dance that night. She replied by asking if I would like to learn. I agreed. So then she taught me by the pool with the moon beaming down on us. Looking back on that night I have to question if my motives were pure or not. Regardless of self-motivation Yah started a new work in me.

As time went on, you could say I moved up in the "ranks" in the congregation. Whether it was because of my looks, age, ability or being a male, I was invited to be part of the established dance troupe. This group was more like the elite people who had power and control over the congregation. As I grew older, I understood what had happened to this dance group and the congregation. Right in front of my eyes the congregation became a house of idolatry. Sin was everywhere I turned, from adulterous affairs to manipulation and the evil tongue (gossip), and in the midst of this mess was me.

While Satan was having a field day with the minds of the people, I was blessed and privileged to meet a gentleman who would mentor and teach me one of the most important lessons in life; that was to love. This love is to love with an everlasting love, the same love that Yahshua bestowed upon His people. Even though I was literally going through hell, Abba blessed me with a mentor and a friend, someone I could look up to; who then would teach me one of the most precious gifts that Abba could offer. This was and still is Yahshua's love.

The truth was revealed one night about the congregational leader and the dance troupe. My very own friends and people, who told me I was like a son to them, were the ones who were spreading rumors and character assignation attempts. The very same people who said they would never hurt me, did, and were proud that they did so. I cried out to the Father asking why, why did this have to happen. My very own team had turned their backs on me. To this day, when other people call them the "hatchet team" I still defend and love them.

With all the garbage that was going on, Yah reminded me to keep dancing and praising Him, and He would deliver me from my foes and tear down the house of Ba'al. Night after night I prayed and waited till Yah gave me the release to leave. During this transition period I was in a difficult place. Abba started to do new things in my life. I was on my own; Abba called my mentor who is my brother in the Lord, to a new city. What was I going to do? Abba knew. He took care of me, through the trials and tribulation, Abba blessed me. Blessing upon blessing He sent my way. He already had begun to build a new relationship, which I did not see. I now had a brother but then He brought me a sister.

When she came to the congregation she was shy and did not want to come and dance in the worship service. For some reason the troupe did not want outsiders to participate in the dance with them, they wanted the worship service to be all for themselves. Self-motivation and pride will get us into trouble. When I saw her, I had seen the glory of Yah radiating from her. I asked myself "who is that woman" (little did I know she would be the one who would be the co-author of the book, you now hold in your hands). I was watching her as she was peering into the isle as she was worshiping though dance prophetically. During one service I went up to her and invited her to dance in the circle. Inviting new people to dance in the service was really not permitted. I may have overstepped my bounds, but I had no choice. The Ruach led me to approach Tina. This was strange since I was a very shy person. I had to respond with the prompting of the Ruach. From there our relationship grew. I have a brother and now a sister in the LORD. I was truly blessed!

Over the years, she taught me to be bold and confident and to stand on the word of Yahweh and His promises.

The power of dance will change an individual forever. Through dance we will become over comers. Tina Clemens also has a story to tell about the power of dance. She has become an over comer through her worship to her Heavenly Bridegroom.

Tina's Story:

"People often ask me how long I've been dancing. Well, I've been dancing since I was a little girl. My childhood home seemed to always be filled with music. My father loved the opera so I grew up on Madame Butterfly and show tunes like "The King and I," "Carousel," "Show Boat," and "Westside Story." It seems like ever since I can remember I have been swaying to the music. My father had quite a record collection, so of course I started my own collection before I was ten years old.

My younger sister started taking ballet lessons when she was about eight years old, while I had opted to take up the clarinet. It turned out that, even though I loved music, playing in the school band was not my cup of tea. I could see the thrill my sister was enjoying taking dance and I approached my father to see if he would be too terribly disappointed if I swapped the clarinet for dance. He gave his approval and I was off to find the joy of my life.

To my horror, I was not naturally gifted in dance. Ballet was far too strict for me. I could see that jazz dance was a much more freer style of dance, which fit my personality far better. So, I switched to jazz. Jazz really connected with something deep within. I did not have a relationship with God at this point in my life, but there was something happening to me when I danced which I loved and I was hooked.

While dancing in shows as a teen, I was always put in the back row, since I was not that good. In order for us less than talented dancers to feel like we were really contributing, the instructor gave us non-important bit parts. I always knew I didn't get a good part because I was not that good. It hurt.

Dance continued to be extremely important in my life. When I attended college, I choose a major in chemistry and a minor in dance. Taking modern dance for the first time, I could now add it to my dance talents. Modern dance I really liked. I could express myself even more with this style. I was learning a lot, getting coached and actually improving my skill. Finally I felt like I was somebody.

My later-to-be husband made the decision for me not to pursue my dance career. He said I would be away from home all the time causing stress on the family. At the time that seemed like the right decision, so I quit my dance dreams. Or so it seemed.

Yet I continued to dream of dance. I devoured every movie with dance while I took classes at the Junior College and local studios whenever I could. During one modern dance class at the JC in 1977, we were asked to choreograph a solo dance for our final exam. I choose the song "Jesus, Lover of My Soul." I forget the artist, but I danced that dance with all my soul and finally I was satisfied.

I knew that the desire to dance was put there by my Creator from the time I first heard music and would sway to the rhythm. Little did I know then that the desire was deposited only to worship Him. From the time I surrendered my will to My Master, I would worship Him to the sound of music. I would dance in my living room for hours and hours and never get tired. For me, I could connect with the Lover of my soul through dance. No one had to tell me to do this; it was just natural to me. I could express my deepest feelings through dance. I could soar and I could fly! I became ONE with my Creator.

It wasn't until 1993 that I danced in the public worship setting. The LORD had hooked me up with another sister who had traveled a similar dance route as I had. Hope and I would dance for hours in her living room worshiping the LORD. I was amazed my joy could be doubled by worship dancing with another who loved the LORD like me.

After a little while of Hope and I dancing together, the LORD had us dance in the congregation worship service where we attended. Bondages began to be broken off people. Many were getting set free. The Spirit of God was moving in mighty ways during the worship times there.

One Sunday, Hope and I began to dance down different aisles of the church. I could see her out of the corner of my eye and noticed we were moving exactly the same way. I mean, it looked like she and I had rehearsed this dance because it was perfectly in sync. Of course we had not rehearsed it at all. This dance was completely Spirit-led and spontaneous. I was so excited and nervous. I hoped I would not make a mistake! After that powerful Sunday, we never danced there again.

To our horror, we were banned from dancing. In fact, I was banned from prophesying, praying or even participating in any church activity. This ban would stay in force until I would submit to letting the elders and pastor lay hands on me to cast out the demon, which so they said, possessed me! I had never been so shocked in all my life! During a meeting with the leadership I was slandered, ridiculed and spiritually wounded (to put it mildly). I wanted to cry out in pain. But my LORD kept whispering in my ear, "Just don't say a word."

The events that followed would fill another book! I can say our LORD Jesus (which I called Him then) became my Hero and ministered to me in the most fantastic ways, which even to this day, I am blessed beyond measure. He had sent me to that congregation to minister in the dance and set people free. When this began to happen the enemy of our LORD got shook up and began to tell lies about us. Because Abba taught me the valuable lesson to walk in love and forgiveness, He has been able to use me in many other situations since then in the area of dance for His glory.

Needless to say, what people say about me does not rock me. When I know I'm walking in the Spirit, people can say whatever they wish and I can still love them.

How I Met Chester

I had been led to study the Hebrew roots of Christianity in 1984 on TV from Joseph Good. I was like a sponge. I just couldn't get enough. Always loving the Old Testament, learning about my roots was easy; it was like feeding carrots to a horse. I just ate it up.

Joseph Good would always recommend attending a Messianic congregation. Well, in 1984 there was not that many available. Whenever I would move to a different town I would hunt, in vain, for a Messianic congregation. Finally we moved to Florida in January of 1997. I was not in Crystal River, Florida a month before I saw the ad in the paper for the Messianic congregation in the next town. I drove 1 hour and saw for the first time what I later learned was Messianic dance.

Not having any experience in Messianic dance I did my own style of dance in the aisle at the synagogue during worship that night. I wanted so badly to join the circle. I eagerly watched yet could hardly keep my feet from running up front to where the circle was dancing. Later that evening one of the dancers, a young man, introduced himself to me, it was Chester. He could see I wanted to dance. He offered to show me the dances, but I was too embarrassed. I was amazed he was so nice to me and extended himself to me, a stranger. I was impressed.

Praying that next week, I felt the LORD wanted me to get together with Chester at the next meeting. Sure enough, he had remembered me and we exchanged phone numbers. That was the beginning of a sweet and special friendship we have enjoyed ever since. The LORD has caused our relationship to grow and mature over these past four years. When I met Chester I did not know even one circle dance. All I knew about dance was my formal dance classes and my free style worship dance. I was eager to learn and Chester was eager to teach.

The first year I watched Chester dance I knew he was going to go far in his dance anointing. I knew Abba had big plans for Chester and I prayed I could help him along the way. I could see Abba had far bigger plans for Chester than dancing in a circle. I have watched him expand his giftings in dance and in the Word.

When Chester approached me about writing this book, I immediately bore witness to it in my spirit. Of course, I didn't let him know this right away, since I wanted to pray about it. I have learned to walk slowing with the LORD and wait for peace, so that I can follow after it. I would not attempt to write a book with any one unless I was ONE with them. Chester and I are ONE in spirit.

Final Thoughts

There will be challenges, which can stand in the way preventing Ephraim and Judah from worshiping as echad. We will need to recognize these challenges and let the Father lead us in His unity. Walking in unity with our brothers will guide us in our worship with and to the Father. While we are worshiping Him, remember how King David worshiped Him. We also can use halal and yadah praise, which will aid us in our worship experience. Let us put on our very own light and sound show for our King. Try it out!

Through my experiences of dance, sin, people, and over coming Egypt I just want to encourage you all to be bold and to go forth and praise the Almighty Creator. Yah has brought me through all my trials and tribulations, and even though I make mistakes, He continues to love me whole-heartedly. The Power of dance is unbelievable. It can shake Satan and his people down to the bone. So be encouraged in your dance. Be blessed as you dance.

All Israel Dances Toward The Tabernacle

Part Three

Holy of Holies

9

The New Yerushalayim
The Holiest of Holies

N ow that we have progressed further into our worship experience, let us enter into the Holiest Place of all.

The Tent of Meeting erected in the wilderness under the direction of Moshe/Moses was a copy of the original one in heaven. YHVH showed Moshe the real thing. How magnificent it must be! The Holiest of Holies is a room with specific dimensions, which we find listed in Exodus 37:1-9. The planks of acacia-wood, being the walls of the Holy Place, were overlaid with gold. There was no light in the Holiest Place, for the only article of furniture was the Ark with the Mercy Seat on top of it, with two Cherubs; one from the end at one side and one from the end at the other.

There was no light in the Holiest Place for the Sh'khinah was it's only Light. The High Priest was privileged to enter into the Holy of Holiest Place once a year and then only with the blood of the Lamb. He would die for failing to follow the directions that Yah had set; he must not come whenever he wants (Leviticus 16:2) and he must wear the correct garments (Exodus 28:43).

Let us feast our eyes on the picture of the future Holiest Place. The New Yerushalayim comes down from heaven, where it awaits its presentation. John, the Revelator describes this scene. He sees the Holy City, prepared like a bride beautifully dressed for her husband.

"And I heard a loud voice from the throne saying, 'Now the dwelling of God is with men, and he will live with them. They will be his people, and God himself will be with them and be their God. He will wipe every tear from their eyes. There will be no more death or mourning or crying or pain, for the old order of things has passed away'" (Revelation 21:34, NIV).

Starting in the ninth verse until the end of the chapter, John is given a closer look at the Bride, the Wife of the Lamb. We are told the city is of pure gold, as is the city's main street. The city is measured as a square of 1500 miles; gold walls are 216 feet and pearled gates inscribed with twelve tribal names. The foundations of the city are decorated with precious stones reminding us of the High Priest's breastplate of judgment (Exodus 39:8-21).

There is no temple in the New Yerushalayim for Adonai Tzva'ot is its Temple, as is the Lamb (Revelation 21:1-5). There is no need for the sun or moon to shine, for Yah's Sh'khinah gives it light, and its Lamp is the Lamb.

The Holy of Holies Moving Day

Light bulbs should be going off in our heads by now, as we see this picture taking form. The Holiest of Holy Place has moved from heaven to earth since the presence of Yah is with man (Revelation 21:3). The New Yerushalayim is the Holy Place expanded to fit every 'priest' in His kingdom. There is no other article of furniture in the new Holy of Holies. We find no altar of incense, no table for Bread of His Presence (table of Shewbread).

Only the pure can enter, the ones whose names are written in the Lamb's Book of Life. In the old order of things, there was only one priest who could officiate in the Holy of Holies. He was born into the priesthood of Levites and trained to carry out his duties perfectly. He was as pure as humanly possible. However, he was a mere type of the Perfect High Priest, Yahshua Who is Pure and able to make others pure when they drink of His sinless blood.

The high priest presented on his shoulders and heart the tribes of Israel represented by precious stones on His garment of splendor and dignity.

"As you come to him, the living Stone-- rejected by men but chosen by God and precious to him--you also, like living stones, are being built into a spiritual house to be a holy priesthood, offering spiritual sacrifices acceptable to God through Jesus Christ" (1 Peter 2: 4-5 NIV).

The sanctuary in heaven is called the Tent of Witness in the Complete Jewish Bible. This translation is interesting since the sanctuary is the place from which judgments are being proclaimed. The miskhan/tent in the wilderness was the place Yah met with Moshe to conduct the business of the Nation of Israel. We see Yah as our Righteous Judge.

Even the time of the revealing of the two temples is paralleled. The Tent of Meeting in the wilderness was set up on the first day of the first month (Exodus 40:1). The New Yerushalayim was brought down on the first, since the voice said the old order is passed away (see above). This day is the beginning of the eternal future.

"For the cloud of Hashem would be on the Tabernacle by day, and fire would be on it at night, before the eyes of ALL OF THE HOUSE OF ISRAEL" (Exodus 40:38, TSET).

Wow! The last verse and chapter of Exodus reveals another prophetic scene of the present day house of Israel (Judah and Ephraim). Do we have the cloud of Hashem/The Name covering us during the day? What about His waves of Fire as night draws near? His cloud and His magnificent fire consume us as we dance as the Tabernacle. We are Israel and the dancing Tabernacle, in which our Soul Yah resides in.

What Is the Priest to Do in the New Yerushalayim?

"No longer will there be any curses. The throne of God and of the Lamb will be in the city, and his servants will worship him. They will see his face, and his name will be on their foreheads … And they will reign forever and ever" (Revelation 22:35, CJB).

A husband is to come into his bride and abide with her. Now Yah's presence will be with His people. His people have been made up into a 'living house' for Him to dwell. The gold of the New Yerushalayim is the purified saints refined in the Refiner's Fire of love. Only the pure can enter the New Holiest of Holy Places, the New Yerushalayim/Jerusalem.

We, as His priests, will serve Him, our Husband, with worship. We have the privilege, as well, to co-reign with Him in His new Kingdom. Let us peer into the Holy of Holies to see the worship taking place here.

Holy of Holies

10

Circularity of Israel

We have entered into the Outer Court, gone through the Inner Court, now we press on toward the Holy of Holies. What will our beloved Father have in store for us as we enter into the Holy of Holies?

Circularity

The Circularity of Israel through dance is a complex idea, which elaborates on harmony, unity, and circles. With this idea we will see how Yahweh binds harmony, unity, and circles together to form the Circularity of Israel. *Webster's* dictionary defines circle/circularity as follows:

1. In geometry, a plane figure comprehended by a single curve line, called its circumference. Every part of the circle, which is equal distant from a point called the center. Of course all lines drawn from the center to the circumference of periphery, are equal to each other.

2. An assembly surrounding the principal person. Hence any company, or assembly.

In a circle there is no beginning and no end, in which every point is equally distant from a point within the center. Now that we know what a circle is, let's see what was really happening as Miryam/Miriam led the women of Israel into a circle dance. Of all the ways that we can praise the Father, why did Miryam choose to lead the women in a circle dance? One might suggest that it shows unity, and harmony.

Foundation of Dance

A lot of people have the belief that ballet is the foundation of the dance. We like ballet; it is a wonderful way to stretch our muscles and our mind. Ballet is an art form of theatrical dance. Scripture tells us that the children of Israel danced a circle dance. Circle dances need little or no training to do. Unlike the circle dance, ballet is the training and discipline of the body. Ballet training establishes correct posture and positions for dance. Although this training is good, we can worship the Father without becoming a ballet student.

The people of Israel had no training in ballet. Ballet can be dated back to 1581 with the performance of the ballet "Comique de la Royne at the Palais du Petit Bourbun" in Paris. This is known as the birth of ballet, making this art form the youngest of the performing arts. The children of Israel danced four thousand years ago, and they did it without ballet training.

There needs to be clarification on the statement that ballet is the foundation of all dances. It could very well be that ballet is the foundation of dance in our "modern time." I have been studying ballet under an excellent teacher for the past couple of years. Through her, I have opened my worship experience to many forms. I have enjoyed ballet so much, and that I taught my own team ballet. After you read this chapter you will see that ballet training is not necessary to worship the Father.

Mechowlah and Machowl

As Miryam was leading the women in a dance, she guided them in a circle dance. *Strong's* #H4246 is mechowlah (mekh-o-law), dance with a company of people. This word is feminine plural. Mechowlah is used eight other times in scripture to define circle dance as a company of people (Exodus 15:20; 32:19; Judges 11:34; 21:21; 1 Samuel 18:6; 21:11; 29:5; Jeremiah 31:3). Mechowlah is derived from the word machowl, and can be traced back to the word Abel Mechowlah that means meadow of dancing. Another Hebrew word for circle dance is machowl (maw-khole), *Strong's* #H4234. Machowl means to dance in a circle and should not be confused with mechowlah. Although they are very close, mechowlah is used for a company of people, and machowl is the base word for circle dance. Five times in scripture machowl is used (Psalms 30:11; 149:3; Jeremiah 31:12; Lamentations 5:15). Machowl is derived form the word chuwl.

Chuwl (khool) or Chiyl (kheel) *Strong's* #H2342 – a primitive root; to twist or whirl in a circular or spiral manner, to dance. Figuratively to bring forth, drive away, fall grievously with pain or to birth. Chuwl is an interesting word for dance because figuratively it means to bring forth, and even to birth. Have we ever been in a situation where Abba has instructed us to bring forth a message through dance? If He has, we would be participating a type of Chuwl dance. Get it? Chuwl or Cool dance!!

Let us refer back to Exodus 15:20, as Miryam led the women in a circle dance. Their dance circle lays out the format and circularity of a united Israel. The children of Israel were coming out of Egypt with a very scattered identity and with no sense of a united nation. The dance of Miryam depicts the first time they came together as one. When a circle dance is accomplished, all parts of the circle depend on each other. Once unity is created, a likeness of minds is established. Each member of the circle will depend on his or her partners to do their appointed duty. This is the first picture that has been shown to us about the circle dance.

As we know, our Father is the center of everything in existence; around the Father is His creation. We are encircling our Father, He is our center and there is none else. Let us refer back to the second meaning of circle, which means assemblies of people: "An assembly surrounding the principal person. Hence any company, or assembly."

Is that not awesome? Who would have thought that circle also means assemblies? The Father is our principal Person and we are the assembly surrounding Him! He had this plan from the beginning that we all are truly echad (one) with Him. The Father brought the assembly of Israel out of bondage to unite as one. As we dance in a circle we must remember Who is in our center. We, as the children of Israel, are encircling the Father as we dance. Our eyes are not on ourselves. However, all eyes are upon Him Who gave us the breath of life.

We now will see the Father calls Israel His assembly.

"You are to keep it until the fourteenth day of the month, and then the entire assembly of the community of Israel will slaughter at dusk" (Exodus 12:6, CJB).

Strong's #H6951 for assembly is qahal (kaw-hawl), assembly, company, congregation, multitude. This word is derived from #H6950 qahal (kawhal), a primitive root, to convoke, assemble selves together, gather.

In the New Covenant/New Testament we find the same word qahal (assembly) from the Tanach/Old Testament is translated to ekklesia (ek-klay-see'-ah). *Strong's* #G1577 – a calling out, a popular meeting, a religious congregation, assembly, church. We see that Yah has continued His plan with circles and assemblies from the "Old" to the "New" Covenant. For more information on qahal and ekklesia see the book *Who is Israel?* by Batya Wootten, pages 5-7, 82.

"Don't you know? Don't you hear? Have not you been told from the start? Don't you understand how the earth is set up? He who sits above the circle of the earth-or whom its inhabitants appear like grasshoppers-stretches out the heavens like a curtain, spreads them out like a tent to live in" (Isaiah 40:21-22, CJB).

Dancing Wind

This next word, circuit, also explains what a circle is. Circuit – The act of moving or passing round; as periodical circuit of the earth round the sun, or of the moon round the earth; to move in a circle to go around. Psalms 19:6 speaks of Yah's circuit. We can take this picture a step further and say we are His circuit, and we are figuratively and literally dancing around our Father's throne room. "His going forth is from the end of the heaven, and his circuit unto the ends of it, and there is nothing hid from the heat thereof" (KJV). When creation was unfolding into existence we see the Father likes to use circuits. He has everything in its precise order according to His rules of the universe.

Even the wind runs in the circuit the Father has established. "The wind goeth toward the south and turneth about unto the north, it whirleth about continually, and the wind returneth again to His circuits" (Ecclesiastes 1:6, KJV). The KJV chose to use the word whirleth or whirl in Ecclesiastes 1:6 passage. This is interesting because "whirl" is defined as turning with rapidity or velocity, or with circumvolution. Another example would be a whirl of a top, or a whirl of time.

The Hebrew word that is used for whirl in the above passage is halak, (Ecclesiastes 1:6), meaning to walk, in a variety of applications literal and figuratively. Also meaning to march and to whirl. Marching and whirling can be associated with dance. The Hebrew word karar (kaw-rar) *Strong's* #H3769, means to dance and whirl about, like David did in 2 Samuel 6:16. Chagag (khaw-gag) *Strong's* #H2287 is also a word that is used for dance.

Chagag means to move in a circle, to march in a sacred procession, to observe a festival, celebrate, and dance.

We are now able to see how the Father uses His circuits with dance. The wind is literally twirling and dancing around its circuit. Imagine for a moment that the wind becomes the praise and worship leader. Being the leader, the wind leads the trees into worship. The wind becomes the one that encourages or leads the trees to praise. As the wind blows through the trees, the branches start to worship the Father. Next time you are outside, feel the wind blow, imagine the wind is dancing and twirling around you to praise the Father! As you look up with the wind blowing against your face, you will see that the trees and the wind are worshiping the Father with you.

Unity

Before we learn what the definition of unity is, we must understand its preface. The preface uni means having but only one. Yachad (yakh-ad) is the Hebrew word for unity. In the Psalms, *Strong's* #H3162 uses yachad for unity.

Yachad from #H3161 a unit – alike all at once, both, likewise, only together, with all. #H3161 – primitive root to be (or become) one: join unite.

"Behold, how good and pleasant it is for brethren to dwell together in unity." Psalms 133:1 (KJV)

There are several words that use the preface *uni*. Webster's dictionary defines them as follows:

1. Unity – a being united, harmony, agreement
2. Uniform – never changing, all alike
3. Unify – make into one
4. Unite – put together as one, combine, join together
5. Universe - space and all the things in it, the world itself.

As we can see from the definitions, unity is a word for one. A valid interpretation of unity would be taking multiple beings or objects to unite them as one. We can look to the word universe to understand that since the beginning of time we have always been One in His hand.

Even all of the planets and stars dance around the universe! The planets run in their own circuit, moving around the sun. We can watch the sun in our universe to see the parallel to the identity of the Father. All the planets in our solar system are moving in their circuit around the sun. The sun projects its energy to the planets thereby producing life. The picture of the sun is similar to our Father setting forth His glory to shine upon His people. Of course, the light of His glory is far greater than that of the sun. The Father's glory will be our light in His future city. Have we seen the Father's light? As we are upon the Earth we need to let ourselves be wrapped in His glory. If we are wrapped in His glory then His light will shine through us. Could this be the same way it will work in the New Jerusalem? We will be consumed in His glory radiating from us lighting up His city.

"And His city had no need of the sun, neither of the moon, to shine in it. For the glory of God did lighten it, and the lamb is the light thereof" (Revelation 21:23, KJV).

The Father is looking for unity as we dance. He has united His people to be one. When we talk about having unity while we dance we are referring specifically to the circle dance. What could happen if there is not unity among dancers? Remember, without unity there is chaos. The opposite or antonym of unity is disarray. Disarray means disorder, confusion, and loss of regular order. For example a door could be opened for Satan to come in and possibly have legal ground among dancers, if unity is not kept. With legal ground Satan will bring confusion within the dance circle. Can you picture a circle dance with every dancer going in a different direction and doing his/her own thing? Unity must be kept with all dancers while dancing; we have to unite as one against our enemy.

If not he (Satan) will unite with his demons to destroy the people of Yah.

Harmony

While worshiping in a circle, dancers must have unity and harmony. Harmony is what stabilizes order in the heavens, universe and earth. Without harmony there is chaos. All believers form the body of the Messiah and we each have our part to play in His world. What is harmony?

Harmony is the just adaptation of parts to each other in any system or composition of things, intended to form a connected whole; as the harmony of the universe, musical concord, agreement. Equality and correspondence are the causes of harmony.

Genesis 1:1 tells us that God created the heavens and the earth. With this, creation began the harmonious flows of the universe. As our Father created, He spoke with harmony and unity. When the Father was creating, it could have been a musical adaptation with harmony! Just imagine that philharmonic sound! When an average person like you or I speak it sounds harsh regardless of how soft-spoken we are. On the other hand, as we sing, we begin to harmonize with our surroundings and ourselves.

Could we even go so far as to picture that creation may have just flowed from His mouth, or even danced out of it? Go ahead; let yourself picture this! With this view in mind, it gives us a different perspective at the creation scene. Let's try to picture creation flowing so smoothly from His lips.

Adonai instructs Moshe in Deuteronomy 31:19 to write a song and teach it to the children of Israel. This special song is located in chapter Deuteronomy thirty-two. Please read Deuteronomy thirty-two, before you progress to the explanation of the chapter.

We have taken excerpts from *The Chumash* (The Torah with a commentary from the Rabbinic writings), which explains Moshe's song:

"Rabbi Gedaliah Schorr explained that "song" implies the concept of harmony, in that people recognize that all elements of the universe fuse in carrying out God's will, just as the notes in a score of a complex song, all the instruments of an orchestra, and all the voices in a choir join in harmonious cooperation to create a song, as opposed to the disjointed noise that results from the failure of the notes instruments, and voices to harmonize properly." "Since the nature of the song is to express recognition of total harmony of creation, it often mixes past, present, and future, for everything revealed to the prophet as a total reality in which there is no conflict, and which future and past events are not only in harmony, but clarify one another. Thus everything is, melted as if it were all happening at the same time" (pg. 1097,1100: Copyright 1998, 2000, Mesorah Publications, Ltd.).

What other familiar words do we associate with harmony? We have found several words that are useful to help us identify harmony in its entirety. Webster's dictionary defines the following words.

♦ Rhythm – periodical emphasis in a verse or music, metrical movement; harmony; rhyme
♦ Music – melodious harmony, the meter verse, the science of harmonious sounds
♦ Tune – short air of melody, harmony, frame of mind, mood

These words all pertain to harmony. Rhythm, music, tune all have within them something that will unite themselves to be one, or in harmony. Even the word tune itself can be described as a type of dance. Now that harmony has been established we can connect it to unity and dance. We see that circle (dance), unity, and harmony are all equal parts to each other, which in turn creates the Circularity of Israel. Without one the others could not exist properly. When harmony is lacking, unity will not prevail, just as if unity did not coexist with harmony, circle will fail.

Harmony is the basis of music and dance; without harmony there is no concord.

Worship Circles Transcend Space and Time

Unity, harmony, and circle are all clues on what the Father has planned for us. The plan of the Father surpasses space and time. Our brain can vaguely comprehend what is forthcoming. This is my theory on the connection of worship through or in circles. There are three levels of worship to the Father.

1. Earth: Ruach/Spirit was sent for us as our Comforter. Ruach has been on this earth since it was created (Genesis 1:2). People on earth form the first level of the worship circle through the dance.

2. Space: Yahshua is the atonement for our sins and connects us to the Father. The second level of the worship circle is made up of all the planets and the stars. They are worshiping through dance in their circuit, as they circulate around their 'dance floor.'

3. Heaven: Yahweh our Father the ultimate Creator. He sits on His throne. With His breath He gave us life. This is the third and most powerful level of the worship circle to the Father. Here we have all the heavenly beings worshiping at His throne room for all eternity.

This scene is continuous worship to the Father. The three levels are sitting upon each other, earth, space, and heaven. Worship from the earth and space, then the heavens all transcend to the Father. This scene is multidimensional; try to picture it. This worship is full of colors, movements and sounds. WOW! Have this image in your mind the next time you worship Abba and see how it affects your worship experience.

Twelve Tribal Gates

For those who endure to the end, we will be privileged to enter into The City that the Father has made for us, the Heavenly Yerushalayim/Jerusalem. We catch a glimpse of this City in the book of the Revelation.

"Blessed are they that do His commandments, that they may have the right to the tree of life, and may enter in through the gates of the city" (Revelation 21:14, KJV).

"And [the city] had a wall great and high, and had twelve gates, and at the gates twelve angels, and names written thereon, which are the names of the children of Israel. On the east three gates; on the north three gates; on the south three gates; on the west three gates" (Revelation 21:12-13, KJV).

We have a birthright to grasp, enabling us to rise up to meet our destiny to be one with our Father. He has had this planned since the beginning of time. What choice will you make? Will you enter the City, and grasp your birthright or be absent when He checks the Lamb's book of life? Yah has given us the choice. Harmony, unity, and dance will be the only way Ephraim and Judah will be restored. Equality and correspondence on both sides will lead Israel to be reestablished with each of the twelve parts.

As we approach the twelve gates of the Heavenly Yerushalayim we will see that our Bible was not a fairy tale but a blue print for the way we should live our lives. Gazing at our new home we will remember all the trials and persecutions, which we suffered through, realizing it was worth it all. All the promises that Yah made to the people of Israel will be fulfilled. He will take His Bride Israel to His innermost chambers. He has come for His Bride at last! He is our Groom, and a gentleman to His Bride. Our loving, gentle, and caring Bridegroom anxiously awaits His eager Bride at her gate to her prepared city.

How will you be found waiting in line? Will you be leisurely standing by and placid? Or will you be singing, dancing, and shouting that you have made it home! He has fulfilled His promise and united Israel!

When the twelve gates are established in their order, we find the figure forms a circle like a compass; three gates east, three north, three south and three west. This harmonious shape displays to us the completed circularity of Israel. It is magnificent! Having all twelve gates equally forming a circle, will lead us into the city to see our King (Revelation 21:12-13, Ezekiel 48:30-34).

When we see the twelve tribal gates we will know that we have reached our destination to the New Jerusalem. Everything Abba has said and promised will be completed. What is the circularity of Israel? The circularity of Israel is when circle, unity and harmony are positioned correctly to establish His new kingdom, the New Jerusalem. We have seen that the Father uses circles in a variety of applications. Circles are used through dance, assemblies, circuits, and even His New Jerusalem. Through His circles of worship and praise we will see the union of Ephraim and Judah. The union of Ephraim and Judah will show us the Circularity of a United Israel!

II

Ostentatious Worship

hir haShirim is the Hebrew title for the book we have grown to love, even if we admit we have a difficult time figuring it out, the Song of Solomon/Song of Songs. The literal translation is the Song of Songs, indicating it is the song above all songs and there is none other. Rabbi Akiva (135 C.E.) said of the Song, " ... for the whole world is not worth the day on which the Song was given to Israel; for all the writings are holy, but the Song is the holiest of the holy."

We shall examine a passage from the Song to help us see the picture of the Body of Messiah as a worshiping Bride. The bride is depicted in the Shulamite woman, who is the object of the lavish, intoxicating love of her Shepherd/Lover. Notice how he is the one who always comes to visit her; she does not come to him. She spends her life waiting for him, for his direction.

The Song is full of extravagant and elegant poetry. It paints for us an idealistic scene of springtime, innocent love between two lovers with no thought of perpetuating the family name, with no motive but pleasure. Their only goal is to enjoy each other. They are fanciful, playful and transparent.

Having read the previous chapters; we have traveled through the Outer Court, passed through the Holy Place, or the Inner Court, finally arriving to our destination; the Holy of Holies. The worshiping Bride is in for the worship experience of her life. In this place, there are no rules. Let us see what she is like.

Dance of the Two Camps

In Jay P. Green Sr.'s translations of the Interlinear Hebrew-Greek-English Bible (Hendrickson Publishers, Second and Revised Edition, 1984), we find:

"... that we may gaze upon you! What will you see in the Shulamite as the dance of the two camps how beautiful are your footsteps in sandals O prince's daughter" (Song of Songs 7:1).

Since Hebrew is not written with any punctuation, some was intentionally left out here to cause us to ponder the sentence structure.

As we read our literal translation, we notice the Hebrew word we learned in the previous chapters, machanayim (makh-an-ah'-yim) (*Strong's* # H4264, meaning, two camps). We saw how Ya'akov/Jacob witnessed two groups of dancing angels at that place, and now we watch the beautiful Shulamite as she dances in the same place over a thousand years later (the date of the Song is post exile, around 3rd century BCE). In our day we look at this 'place,' not as a literal place, but a spiritual one. Remember that the Song of Songs should be treated as an allegory. It is a story that overflows with metaphor.

The Shulamite depicts the Bride of Messiah and her Shepherd/Lover is Yahshua. We see her as a dancing Bride, one who is radiant, and who is longing for her Lover. One translation of the word shulamite, means "complete, perfect one." She is the responder/receiver of His limitless love.

What Do We See?

We shall focus on the Song of Songs 7:1, plus two verses from chapter six. Staying with the literal translation,

"Beautiful are you O My love, as Tirzah, comely as Jerusalem awesome as bannered armies" (vs 6:4).

"Who is this who looks down as the dawn, fair as the moon, pure as the sun awesome as bannered (armies)" (vs 6:10).

'Awesome' is *Strong's* word # H366 and comes from an unused root word meaning to frighten; frightful; -terrible. 'Bannered' is #H1713 a primitive root; to flaunt, example, raise a flag; figurative to be conspicuous. Now we place these definitions into the verses. Notice, there is no wording found that translates as army, nor is there any word found that indicates warfare, or combat. Our key to correct understanding is to remember that machanayim's root word is 'rest in a tent.' This word, 'bannered' has the same root word as 'degel' (banner), which we find in many passages referring, to raising a standard. The word 'nidgalot' found in 6:10, translated as bannered (armies) attests to the fact that by the time of the Song this root had developed new metaphorical meanings no longer associable with the literal 'banner.' Raise high, make conspicuous … this is the meaning the translators Ariel and Chana Bloch use in their translation of the Song of Songs (Randon House, New York, 1995 p. 150,192). For the word 'awesome,' #H366, the Blochs choose the word, daunting. Their choice reflects the awe the ancient Hebrews felt for heavenly bodies such as sun, moon, stars (Ibid, p. 191; also see Judges 5:20).

The Dancing Bride

Webster's Dictionary further paints a vivid portrait of the dancing Bride.

1. Flaunt - to wave, flutter, or move ostentatiously; to display boastfully, brazenly; parade; synonym - brandish.
2. Brandish - wave, shake, flutter (comes from brand + sword).
3. Ostentatiously - unnecessary show, pretentious parade.
4. Pretentious - a claim …any quality or feature that invites or aims to invite admiration or attention; showy
5. Conspicuous - obvious to the eye or mind; manifest attracting attention; striking
6. Daunting - to subdue the courage of; to intimidate

Notice how many of the descriptive words above are words involving movement, as in dance…

Get the picture?!

Bashful Bride

Is she shy? Is she timid? Is she holding back? Does she hide her expression of love for her lover under a bush? No, this Bride is bold, extravagant, even to the point of being unnecessarily showy. She is flamboyant, splashy, 'wave under one's nose' in her demonstration (as in flaunt), plain as day (conspicuous). She is flat out intimidating! She doesn't care who sees her, in fact those who do get to see her urge her onward, "Encore, Encore! Dance again! We love to watch you!" They rejoice in watching this one who is so expressive in her love. They want to see more! She is a beautiful sight to behold. Hers is a dance of unabashed love.

How many times have we been told things like, "Hold it down. Don't get too excited. Don't let your emotions run wild. Be calm and subdued." How often have we been warned not to let this 'religious' thing get a hold on us or get out of hand? If we, both houses of Israel, are the collective Bride of Yahshua, shouldn't we be as ostentatious in our worship as the Shulamite? As we dance and worship and flaunt and get giddy, our Bridegroom is delighted and takes great joy in His Bride. This is the kind of love He has wanted, the kind that burns hot, a fire that cannot be quenched! This is the hot, first-love He requires (Revelation 2:4). "...love...its sparks are a raging fire, a devouring flame. Great seas cannot extinguish love, no river can sweep it away" (Song of Songs 8:6,7).

Connecting the Dots

Remember the game of connect the dots we played in the chapter on Miryam? Since you liked it so well, we shall use it again to make a silhouette of the scene our Yah/God is making for us. Ya'akov first comes to this place and names it Beth El [House of Yah]. He has a dream seeing angels going up and down on a staircase to heaven. "Surely Yah is in this place," he says. This is our first dot. Next, twenty years later, Ya'akov returns to this place where angels meet him. (Could they be the identical angels he saw twenty-years earlier?) This time he renames the place Machanayim. The same night he wrestles with Yah in the flesh (Yahshua), and names the place P'ni-El [face of Yah]. This is our second dot.

The third dot is the ownership of the city of Machanayim. Originally Moshe/Moses had given the city to the tribe of Gad as an inheritance. However, since the Levites had no inheritance they went to Y'hoshua/Joshua to ask to be given cities as promised by Moshe. Good ol' Y'hoshua said, 'Sure thing boys!' Well, guess what one of the cities was? That's right, Machanayim (Joshua 13:26-30; 21:38). The exciting thing here is that this place (our spiritual/prophetic place) belongs to not one tribe, but to the priests! Is this getting anyone excited yet?! Since we are called "a kingdom of priests," then Machanayim is for us!

Our fourth dot is the dancing king of Israel, David. When David leaves Jerusalem, fleeing from his son Avshalom/Absalom, he heads for... You guessed it! Machanayim. This place becomes a place of refuge for David and his men. Check out the bounty of goodies they feast on while in Machanayim (2 Samuel 17:24-29).

The House of David finds in Machanayim

♦ rest
♦ refuge
♦ refreshing
♦ restoration

Interesting to note, a wealthy man took care of all David's needs while in Machanayim (2 Samuel 19:32). The final dot is assigned to the toe-tapping, beautiful Shulamite unabashed, daunting and eager to demonstrate the fervor of her first love. Our picture is taking shape; we now have five dots. What do we see?

1. The before, during and after the family split.
2. The prophetic picture (the before)
3. The beginning of the fulfillment (the during); yet abundant provisions for the House of David even during the split
4. The celebrating Bride. (The original "NO FEAR" slogan comes from her!). She's not running or hiding from anything. She has nothing to hide or fear.
5. The last dot we'll connect to the first, bringing us full circle... Angels going and coming from heaven

Machanayim, two camps, is the prophetic picture of the two houses of Israel. The dancing we see being done by the angels on the second dot is now being done by the Bride on the last dot (prophetic fulfillment).

We do not see Machanayim beyond the Song of Songs in our Bibles. The two camps have become ONE in the Shulamite; it is the final dot, the last picture. When Ya'akov had the dream of the stairway to heaven and the angels going and coming, could it have been the promise of the coming revelation of the restoration of the split house in the final days? Are we reaping this joyous revelation today? When he was met with the two camps of dancing angels we see the tragedy of the family split, yet we also see the rejoicing at the promise of the restoration, hence the dancing.

Frightening Sight

Most of our Bible translations will use the word, "terrible or frightful" in Song of Songs 6:4, as noted above. Pondering this choice for a moment, we can see how the confident, celebrating Bride/Shulamite can be "terrible" to look upon. She is frightening to Yah's enemies! The Bride of Messiah is so confident in the love, care, protection and provisions coming from her Lover/King that she is a frightening sight to the enemy. Recall the chapter, "THE DANCING WARRIOR." There, Abba taught us from Isaiah 30:32 that He converts our praise and worship into blows to the enemy. No wonder the enemy is frightful and fearful when he sees the worshiping Bride!

The Bloch's translation uses, instead of terrible or frightening, the word "daunting," to subdue the courage of, to intimidate. Don't you just love that? The enemy has no courage in the face of the confident worshiping Bride. Actually, he is intimidated by her ostentatious worship. The Bride's worship is a wave under the enemy's nose, as if to flaunt her confidence. As the Bride expresses her unabashed love towards her King, she is caught up in His beauty, His holiness, and His power. As she worships, she is unaware of the effects this worship is having in the heart of the enemy! She has no clue! She is carefree!

Holy of Holies Worship

It is in this place, Machanayim, the place of two camps, where Ya'akov, who is soon to be re-named Israel, has reaffirmed to him the promise of the covenant Yah cut with Avraham. The ascending and descending angels open the way into Yah's house. They bring from heaven a revelation of Ya'akov's promised future family, and they take Ya'akov's praise offering back to heaven. Each time Abba sends His Bride to worship at Machanayim, we see more clearly His perfect plan for the restoration of both houses of Israel: Judah and Ephraim.

Machanayim! The place of two camps! Home of the awesome Dancing Bride! Place of Restoration!

Most fascinating is the abundant provisions received by the House of David through a wealthy man while in Machanayim. Bring this into the present day fulfillment as the Body/Bride of Messiah is receiving rest, refuge, refreshment, and restoration while in the place of Machanayim. "The Wealthiest Man" is meeting all of her needs! Abba is in the business of restoring the House of David while the whole house, or Bride is coming into the most joyful, confident phase of her relationship with her Bridegroom. This is Holy of Holies worship. There is no enemy in this place! She intimidates the far removed enemy as she parades her love/worship for all to see. As her trust in her Bridegroom grows, so too does her confidence in His provisions, protection and care. The relationship just keeps getting sweeter and sweeter. Taste and see how good is the LORD!

As the two houses of Israel continue to come together in Abba's glorious restoration blueprint, the Bride will become more ostentatious in her worship. Get ready for great and terrible parades. Prepare yourself to see showy displays of divine love!

Some may say it is "unnecessary," but nonetheless, the undaunted young Bride will just keep tapping her toes and whirl down the rows of on-lookers, her eyes fixed upon her Lover/King!

Ostentatious Worship

12

Dance of Purity

Father, we are here!! We have found your instructions and we have returned. You started us with your Torah (Instructions), gave us your prophets and finally sent your Son Yahshua/Jesus, to seal our name in the Lamb's Book of Life. Oh Father how we yearn for You, yearn to be one with You. Our hearts are crying with a deep passion, to let us return. Even through all our sins and transgressions against You, thank You for letting us return. We have come with our brothers to be with You eternally."

As Believers, we must have the same yearning that our Father has for us (Jeremiah 31:20). Our hearts need to be pure and clean before we can enter into the Holy of Holies. The Father tells us to call out to Him, He will answer and guide us (Jeremiah 33:3). He is Avinu Malkeynu, our Father our King.

Purification - The Only Way

Wrestling with our flesh is a daily process we all must endure. Although it is tough we must strive for perfection through purification. Purification is the act of making oneself clean and pure before God. Yah has given us the dance, and we must strive to operate in this gift from a pure heart. Being pure means we are free from guilt or defilement of sin. We do not refuse to hear the Holy Spirit, the Ruach HaKodesh, if and when He seeks to convict us of error in our lives (John 16:8). We walk in innocence with purity of the heart.

'Perfection through dance' is a difficult concept for many Believers to grasp. Many dancers take the attitude that we do not have to be perfect in our dance because Abba "knows" our heart. How many times have we heard that statement? Or perhaps we have heard people say, "They are such a perfectionist." I must admit that I have said it before. Is it wrong to think this way? Perhaps the way we should look at it is, while Abba does know our heart and our intentions, nonetheless, we, the present-day house of Israel, because of our great love for Him, want to settle for nothing less than bringing before Him a perfect offering.

Being perfect when we worship Abba is also equally important. When we worship whole-heartedly we are striving for perfection. Whether through dance, singing, or teaching we must strive for perfection. What is being perfect when we worship Abba? It is when we know one hundred percent of our worship is directed toward Him. Again, we give the best we can give to Him. If we know within ourselves that Abba is pleased then our worship is perfect in His sight. Our own standards of perfection may not meet other people's standards. However, our standard must meet His standard. Abba makes His standards clear through His Living Word. So I say unto you, perfection only comes through purification. For Yahshua/Jesus says "Therefore, be perfect, just as your Father in heaven is perfect" (Matthew 5:48, CJB). What must we do to have purified and perfected hearts as dancers of the Almighty Spirit God?

Separation Leads Us to Holiness

The world is a place of vile contaminates able to defile the saints of Yah. This is the on-going battle in which we will need His strength to stand against its fearsome attack. First, we must separate ourselves from the activities, which will cause us to fall into sin. Overcoming our flesh is a difficult task if we are already involved in sin. The deeper we fall into sin, the more Yah's anointing will be covered by Satan's darkness. "If, then, the light in you is darkness, how great is that darkness" (Matthew 6:23, CJB). But as we separate from that darkness and open our hearts to God's Living Word, our heart of sin will be filled with His light. Yah's glorious light will pierce through Satan's cloak of darkness. By taking steps to separate ourselves from the world, we are participating in a spiritual open-heart surgery.

Secondly, as we begin to grow in Him and live our lives according to His Living Word, our daily lives will demonstrate that we are the children of Israel. Through the perfected and purified life of the Living Torah, our brothers and sisters will see the change inside of us. They too will want what we have. By honoring Yahweh, He in return will bless us. For separation ultimately leads us to holiness and purity.

To purify oneself before the Father is a necessity. The purification process takes place from within a pure heart. Yahshua/Jesus openly rebuked those who only partook in "ceremonial purification." Those who did so were following manmade traditions. What they taught and spoke looked good from the outside, but their hearts were corrupted with darkness. Since their expressions did not come from a pure heart, their worship was in vain. Yahshua considers this type of "worship" useless in His sight (Mark 7:1-3; Luke 11:39-41; Ephesians 4:28).

"And the LORD said unto him, Now do you Pharisees make clean the outside of the cup and the planter; but your inward part is full of ravening and wickedness. Ye fools, did not he that made that which is without make that which is within also? But rather give alms of such things as ye have; and, behold, all things are clean unto you" (Luke 11:39-41, KJV).

Our Father will bless those who have a pure heart. They will see God (Matthew 5:8). Yah is looking for us to have a type of "Spiritual Purity." Spiritual Purity is the act of knowing Who our Father is, following His Word and keeping ourselves from being contaminated by the world of sin (James 1:27).

Purity

Realizing we are part of the people of Israel leads us deeper into worship and praise to our Father. Knowing we are part of the people of His chosen people helps us to better understand our Father and the plan He long ago laid out for our future. If we do not understand Abba's prophetic picture of the restoration of all Israel, which also is the restoration of His Kingdom, then how close can our walk be with Him? Do we want to know what our God is accomplishing through Israel? To worship the Father in spirit and in truth includes knowing His picture perfect plan for all Israel. Not having a clue about Israel's full re-unification will leave us lacking in our worship and praise to Him. Some may not agree with the last statement. However, if we truly want to worship the Father (Yahweh) the Son (Yahshua) and the Holy Spirit (Ruach) then we need to understand "Israel." The deeper we search and seek Him; the more purity of our worship will be made evident.

"Call to Me and I will answer you, and I will tell you great and mighty things, which you do not know" (Jeremiah 33:3, NASB).

"'You will seek Me and find Me when you search for Me with all your heart" (Jeremiah 29:13, NASB).

Defining Purity

Judah and Ephraim are repenting and Yah is allowing for our return. We will return as His Bride, Bethuwlah Yisrael! We must return to Him in a state of purity. Lets explore more on the definition of purity. *Webster's Dictionary* lays out the foundation:

1. Freedom from guilt or defilement of sin, innocence; as a purity of the heart or life
2. Freedom from contamination by illicit sexual connection
3. Freedom from any sinister in proper views; as the purity of motives or designs

Pure Gifts From Above

The Father has gifted us with many talents and abilities. While we are worshiping together as a unified body, we should not get jealous of each other's gifts. He has given each of us various gifts with which to worship Him. We are not to have any thoughts of malice toward other dancers or worshipers. We must show respect and have pure thoughts concerning everyone if we are to be pure (1 Timothy 4:12, 5:2). Yah has given each of us different anointing for His reasons. We cannot walk in someone else's anointing; the Father will not bless this. Even though we may want someone's anointing, we must wait for the Father to bless us with our own anointing. Everyone has their own unique individual anointing, which the Father placed in our soul when He gave us the breath of life. He will make it bloom from within us till He sees fit to bring it out.

We must keep ourselves from being contaminated by illicit sexual desires! By mastering our physical emotions through our body, our heart becomes pure. Sexual impurities are one of the toughest battles to fight. But the Father has made us stronger than our flesh. We can be the master of our mind and body (sexual impurities) through the Father, or we can become a slave to it. We want to be masters of our minds and our bodies (Matthew 6:24). If we allow Satan to use our "temples" for darkness, then the repercussion will be bondage. The more we are in bondage the thicker the wall will be built around our "temple," which will, in turn, separate us from the Father. Abba desires a union with us that is so intense that it will make us 'one' with Him (Ephesians 6:10). Would you like to be a slave to your own body? No way!!

Remember, Yah has given us freewill. We can choose to sin or to worship Him. When we do slip into sin, we must recognize what we did, and then rectify the problem immediately. Through Him we can overcome any temptation Satan has to offer. If we tune only into the Father as He is speaking to us, then we will have no desire to have sinister or improper thoughts.

We are capable of living a pure life. That is Yah's desire for us. Just how do we live a pure life? We can do the outward things, such as separating ourselves from unclean movies, jokes, magazines, Internet, and television. We can be pure to our "temple" by eating correctly, exercising, resting and making our life holy as possible. We will need to take a heart examination to see that the motivation and the meditation of our heart is pleasing to Yah. Being obedient must be high on the list if we are to live a life of purity.

Dancing As Virgins

Judges twenty-one tells us the story of what happened when the people did not assemble before God. The Judge of Israel commanded all the camps and tribes to assemble before Adonai. Of all the towns, the people of Jabesh-gilead were nowhere to be found. For disobeying the law, the soldiers of Israel killed everyone who had sex with a man. The deaths included men, women, and children. We see and learn from chapter twenty-one that the people of Jabesh-gilead were involved in sin.

This area of Israel had a large number of people participating in impure sexual acts. Everyone who had sex with a man was killed. The only survivors of the massacre were four hundred young virgins. Purity saved them. By separating their lives from impure acts, the Father allowed their lives to be saved. Yah saw that these women followed the path of purity; their separation was their life. We must be like these separated virgins as we dance unto the Father; purified and perfected! The Father tells us to repent and give up our wicked ways, and return as a virgin.

"Then the virgin will dance for joy, young men and old men together" (Jeremiah 31:13, CJB).

Strong's #H1330 - Bethuwlah (beth-oo-law) is the Hebrew word used for virgin. It is the feminine past participle of an unused root meaning to separate; a virgin (from her privacy) sometimes (by continuation) a bride: also figuratively a city or state:- maid or virgin. Bethuwlah takes multiple meanings: separate, bride, city/state; all of these words are valid representations of Israel! Then Israel will dance for joy, both young men and old men together. Therefore we can say Israel is the Bride, in fact the Virgin Bride of Yahshua!

Converting Sorrows Into Joy: Jeremiah 31:12

How does the Father convert our sorrows into joy? First, Abba wants us to give our pain and turmoil to Him. He is the Lover of our soul and He wants to take care of us. With total trust and love we offer our pain to Him, which He then converts into joy. The joy Abba gives us we find nowhere else. Further, "The joy of the Lord is our strength" (Nehemiah 8:10, CJB).

The Father is always experiencing joy. And if He is always joyous, and we can always draw our strength from Him, then we too can continue in His joy. No longer holding onto our pain and sorrows, we take the joy He has given us and offer it back to Him. When we offer our joy to Him, the cycle is completed of converting our sorrows into joy!

With this conversion factor we will be able to experience the Father more pleasantly. We will have His joy. With His joy we then will be able to meditate upon Him. Doing so will allow us to know His will which He desires for us.

Meditation of the Heart

If we think only our mouths can meditate then we are fooling ourselves. Our heart is used as a meditation device for the Father! Some suggest our heart is the gateway to our soul. Following this thought we can say our soul meditates on the Father: "Let the words of my mouth and the meditation of my heart be acceptable in your sight" (Psalms 19:14, KJV). The Hebrew word for meditation in this passage is "higgagown," *Strong's* #H1902, higgagown (hig-gaw-gone), murmuring sound, a musical notation (probably similar to the modern affetusso to indicate solemnity of movement) by implications a machination device, meditation, solemn sound.

The Psalmist asks the Father to accept the words of his mouth and the meditation from his heart. When put into perspective we see from *Strong's* word #H1902 that the Psalmist's heart was actually crying out to the Father. His heart was making a solemn sound of praise and worship to the Father.

By meditating from the heart we open ourselves to a deeper intimacy to and with the Father.

Abba looks at our heart to see if it is pure or tainted. He does not judge according to outside appearances, but instead looks inside our heart. Even though we defile our temples with sin, He has sent His son Yahshua as the priest of our temple to clean and wash those sins away with His magnificent blood.

"But Adonai said to Sh'mu'el/Samuel, 'Don't pay attention to how he looks or how tall he is, because I have rejected him. Adonai doesn't see the way humans see – humans look at the outward appearance, but Adonai looks at the heart'" (1 Samuel 16:7, CJB).

We are the temples in which Yah's Spirit dwells. Our heart can be seen as a parallel to the Aron HaKodesh, the Holy Ark, which was placed in the Holy of Holies. We know Abba gave us a perfected pure essence, which we don't even realize we have. He gave us a soul. Our soul is part of God. He gave us part of Himself. Where did he place our soul? In our heart (Aron Hakodesh). The soul is divine since it is part of Abba. The soul/spirit connects with/to Abba and dwells in our Holy Ark. The Father has His silver or crystallized cords which connects us to Him through our soul (Ecclesiastes 12:6). Peering into our heart we will find in there, part of Abba, He is the Divine Essence, which is our soul. Awesome! We have His holy presence in us twenty-four hours a day. If we will allow it, we can have twenty-four hours of non-stop worshiping of our Creator! If we will allow it, or even encourage it, Yah will draw the worship/praise dance from within us. The only question is, what type of worship will we present to the Father?

Dancing From Every Nation

Nations around the world are worshiping the Almighty God. The people are worshiping through dance in a variety of ways. Are we to judge the way different people dance before Abba? After all, not every nation will do the same type of dance to which we might be accustomed. Over the past few years I have been privileged to see many diverse people lifting praise to the Father. I have seen ballet, jazz, messianic, step, modern, Hawaiian, Israeli and Caribbean dancing. Not all of these dance types were circle dances. We all don't have to do circle worship. We've seen in previous chapters how Yah uses the circle dance; but there are a multitude of dance patterns that are acceptable to the Father. What kind of worship/praise dance does Yah want? He wants what comes from the pure heart. If the motivation of our heart is pure while we praise Him, then our worship is acceptable to the Father.

When our worship is not pure, when we have the wrong motivation, then we are playing with fire--because we are committing sin. The first sin is that of lying. The only reason why we should praise dance is to give exultation to the Father first and then to the people, but if there is another reason behind our dance, then we are lying to Abba. With this lie, a form of manipulation is set in motion. We are trying to coerce the people into believing that we are something we are not. Sometimes dancers don't know they are using worship for self-exaltation. They do not realize that what they are doing is self-motivated. That is why it is imperative that we listen to the Spirit of Yah as we seek to worship Him. Let Him tell us who He thinks we are worshiping!

In every nation on Earth there are people dancing before their Creator. They are dancing the way the Spirit leads them. We should not be the stumbling block in somebody's worship. We should not have a judgmental attitude. Instead, we should let "he who is with out sin cast the first stone" (John 8:7). We should "not judge according to appearance," but instead should seek to "judge with righteous judgment" (John 7:24). Perhaps we should even join with them and bind our worship with theirs to create unity and a likeness of minds. Unity between brothers and sisters is what Abba desires. Do we desire what Abba desires? Do we want to enjoy and experience the dance of purity? I will be the first to sign up!!

Israel's Pure Lamb

Experiencing the dance of Purity will only draw us closer to the Lamb, which was a Man (Exodus 12:3). The Lamb Who died for our sins is our beloved Yahshua. When the blood of the Lamb is applied to our heart; we become one with Israel. As we partake and drink the blood, we will bind ourselves to the New Covenant forever. That Man, the One called "the Lamb of God" (John 1:29), also was called "My Servant, Israel" by the Father:

"He said to me, 'You are my servant, Israel, through whom I will show my glory'" (Isaiah 49:3, CJB). Abba called Yahshua Israel. Yahshua was the first Israel, and Ya'akov became the second.

Yahshua (the incarnated God man) gave Ya'akov His title name Israel, after they wrestled all night (Genesis 32:25-33). Can we imagine wrestling all night till daybreak? But were they fiercely fighting? When Yahshua struck Ya'akov in the hip, we can say He was hitting below the belt "because the Man struck Ya'akov's hip at its socket" (Genesis 32:33, CJB).

If you've ever seen a wrestling match then you know what goes on when people wrestle. Sometimes the wrestlers become tangled together all on top of each other, becoming very hard to separate them till the match is over. Finally, the winner is declared. The wrestler, who lost, his title would be given to the winner. This analogy can be compared to Yahshua and Ya'akov's wrestling match. This wrestling match that took place changed the world forever.

Dance of Purity

What is the dance of purity? We see it when we purify ourselves like the virgin Israel, when we are like Yahshua. The dance of purity starts with Ya'akov/Jacob as he "wins" his battle against Yahshua (which was really a battle about Ya'akov being conformed to, wrapped up and intertwined with, the One with whom he wrestled). Ya'akov named the battle site P'ni El, (Genesis 32:8), because he had a pure heart and had nothing to hide from His Lover. He was "face to face" with Him.

Can we imagine what Ya'akov might have seen as he was face to face with God? More likely they were eye-to-eye. What could have Ya'akov been thinking as he gazed into the blazing eyes of fire. It is said that the most intense and passionate time in a person's life is when they consummate their marriage, and come face to face with their lover in intimacy. In reality, the most intense and intimate time is our life should be experiencing Yahshua as the Lover of our soul. It is sad but most men and women are closer to their spouses than with Yah. Yah desires a close and intimate relationship with us. Yet we push Him aside for fleshy desires.

For Ya'akov's purity Yah has given Him the name of purity, the title Israel. This is the first time we see the purity of Israel.

All Israel Dances Toward The Tabernacle

For Ya'akov's purity Yah has given Him the name of purity, the title Israel. This is the first time we see the purity of Israel.

Turn Shulamite Turn

In the Song of Songs we see that the Shulamite bride represents both houses of Israel. The Shulamite has nothing in her heart to hide from her Bridegroom. With a pure heart she can come face to face with her Lover. Now it is her turn to become 'one' with Him; to experience His eyes of fire, and the intensity of His love. This is why she is bold and extravagant with her praise and worship. She knows she has nothing to hide. With the Shulamite representing a completed Israel she takes us back to our first love, to see our Father face to face.

With this progression from the outer-court through the inner-court, and now into the Holy of Holies, we have seen how the Father transforms our body and draws praise and worship out of our temple. Having a pure heart before the Father, and knowing there is only room in our heart for Him and His purposes for our lives, we will see Him Face to Face and be allowed to enter into the Holy of Holies.

We have presented you with a fraction of a story, which hopefully will help guide you into the chambers of Yahweh. We want to enter with innocence in thought and allow Him to mold us into what He wants for our life.

"With the absence of time there is no separation between our Lover and us. As we progress through our life Yah will be with us forever."

C. Anderson

"What is it about You Lord, that makes me want to dance."

J. MacFadder

Dance of Purity

13

Lacking Nothing By Fearing Yah

We must find out how to fear Yah. We must know what fear is. Lack of fear is the key to not lacking anything. Surely all of us would like to be without any needs. So let us see what the fear of Yah is. We shall look into a few scripture verses to see what our Father has to say about fearing Him.

Fear the LORD, you [holy ones] his saints, for those who fear him lack nothing. The lions may grow weak and hungry, but those who seek the LORD lack no good thing (Psalms 34:9-10, NIV).

Come, my children, listen to me; I will teach you the fear of the LORD. Whoever of you loves life and desires to see many good days, keep your tongue from evil and your lips from speaking lies. Turn from evil and do good; seek peace and pursue it (Psalms 34:11-14, NIV).

The Spirit of Yah will teach us to fear Yah. If we fear Him we will...

♦   Keep (guard) our tongue
♦   Do good
♦   Go after shalom

Assemble the people– men, women and children, and the aliens living in your towns– so they can listen and learn to fear the LORD your God and follow carefully all the words of this law. Their children, who do not know this law, must hear it and learn to fear the LORD your God as long as you live in the land you are crossing (Deuteronomy 31:12-13, NIV).

For the LORD your God dried up the Jordan before you until you had crossed over. The LORD your God did to the Jordan just what he had done to the Red Sea when he dried it up before us until we had crossed over. He did this so that all the peoples of the earth might know that the hand of the LORD is powerful and so that you might always fear the LORD your God" (Joshua 4:23-24, NIV).

"Now fear the LORD and serve him with all faithfulness. Throw away the gods your forefathers worshiped beyond the River and in Egypt, and serve the LORD" (Joshua 24:14,NIV).

If you fear the LORD and serve and obey him and do not rebel against his commands, and if both you and the king who reigns over you follow the LORD your God– good! (1 Samuel 12:14, NIV).

The LORD remembers us and will bless us: He will bless the house of Israel, he will bless the house of Aaron, he will bless those who fear the LORD– small and great alike (Psalms 115:12-13, NIV).

Blessed are all who fear the LORD, who walk in his ways. You will eat the fruit of your labor; blessings and prosperity will be yours (Psalms 128:1-2, NIV).

Do not be wise in your own eyes; fear the LORD and shun evil (Proverbs 3:7, NIV).

To fear the LORD is to hate evil; I hate pride and arrogance, evil behavior and perverse speech (Proverbs 8:13, NIV).

Hear this, you foolish and senseless people, who have eyes but do not see, who have ears but do not hear: Should you not fear me?" declares the LORD. "Should you not tremble in my presence? I made the sand a boundary for the sea, an everlasting barrier it cannot cross. The waves may roll, but they cannot prevail; they may roar, but they cannot cross it. But these people have stubborn and rebellious hearts; they have turned aside and gone away. They do not say to themselves, 'Let us fear the LORD our God, who gives autumn and spring rains in season...'" (Jeremiah 5:21-24, NIV).

"Did Hezekiah king of Judah or anyone else in Judah put him to death? Did not Hezekiah fear the LORD and seek his favor? And did not the LORD relent, so that he did not bring the disaster he pronounced against them? We are about to bring a terrible disaster on ourselves!" (Jeremiah 26:19, NIV).

The Holy Scriptures speak for themselves. We find from the above scriptures some insight concerning fear.

- Listen, hear, and carefully follow the words of this law to learn to fear Yah. If we know what His Word teaches and says to us, it will bring the fear of Yah.
- Yah did mighty acts, such as drying up the Red Sea and the Jordan, just so that we would learn to fear Him.
- Fear, service [worship] to Him, obedience (not rebelling) must all go together, but not until we throw away our idols.
- Blessings and prosperity will be ours, if we fear Yah.
- hate evil
- Tremble in His presence.
- Hezekiah feared the LORD, because of that Yah relented.

The word FEAR is *Strong's* #H3372 a primitive root; to fear; morally to revere; caus. to frighten: ... be (make) afraid, dread (ful); put in fear, be had in reverence, see, terrible.

..."they were terrified and fearful as they stood at the foot of the mountain" (Hebrews 12:18-24, NIV).

In Genesis 3:10 Adam and Eve were afraid after they sinned, so they hid from Yah. The fear of Yah is a motive of obedience. The fear of the LORD is a fear CONJOINED WITH LOVE AND HOPE and is therefore not a slavish dread, but rather a dutiful reverence. Yah is called the fear of Isaac, the God who Isaac feared in Genesis 31:42, 53 (Easton's Study Bible, software).

As I looked up the *Strong's* number for fear, my eyes caught the word a few lines below. This word is #H3376 Yiriyayh/Jirijah which is the name (?) given to Yah by Isaac (if not by Isaac, then who, and why did he fear Yah?) meaning "fearful of Yah." This word stems from #H3373 (same as #H3372) and #H3050 (Yah, the LORD most vehement).

Pure

For the LORD God is a sun and shield; the LORD bestows favor and honor; no good thing does he withhold from those whose walk [life] is [PURE] blameless (Ps 84:11, NIV)

Pure is *Strong's* #H8549 from #H8552; entire (literally, figuratively or morally); also (as noun) integrity, truth:

KJV: without blemish, complete, full, perfect, sincerely (-ity), sound, without spot, undefiled, upright(-ly), whole.

Webster defines PURE as separate from all heterogeneous or extraneous matter; without alloy, stain, or taint; clear; unmixed; sheer. Complete; absolute; as pure nonsense. Free from what vitiates, weakens, or pollutes; faultless; as he spoke pure French. Free from moral defilement or guilt; hence innocent; guiltless. Chaste. Ritually clean.

Heterogeneous – differing in kind; having unlike qualities; dissimilar;- opposed to homogeneous.

Extraneous – not essential or intrinsic (belonging to the constitution, nature, or essence, of a thing; independent of that which is contingent or acquired.); foreign; as to separate gold from extraneous matter.

Hetero – different
Homo – same

…"keep oneself from being polluted by the world" (James 1:27,NIV).

If we are as gold in the process of purification, then the contaminates of the world will defile us causing us to be corrupt, polluted, mixed, tainted, unclean and incomplete.

As we study His instructions (this is our 'seeking' of Him), we learn to fear Him. IF we tremble in His presence, we will desire to be pure, without contamination, pleasing Him in all things. By seeking Him we find out what pleases Him. As the Refiner continues His process of refining His gold, we are co-labors with Him in His process. Perhaps we are not as pure as we would like to be nor as pure as we thing we should be by this time in our love-walk with Him. Yet, our hope is in the good work He is accomplishing in our lives. His good work will bring us to completion and we will be that spotless Bride with which He so longs to reign.

We are capable of living a pure life for it is His desire. Just how do we live a pure life? We can do the outwardly characteristics such as being separate from unclean movies, jokes, magazines, Internet and television. We can be pure in our temple service by eating, exercising, resting and working as properly and holy as possible. We will need to take a heart examination to see that the motivation and the meditation of our heart is pleasing to Yah. Being obedient must be high on the list if we are to live a life of purity. Remember pure means without alloy. When learning about the silver fillings in dentistry, I was surprised to discover the silver used is not pure. I learned the silver had many alloys in it, making the silver not really silver at all, but a mix of many different metals. Let us not be a mixed metal, having impurities, but let us be pure with no mixture.

The world is a place of vile contaminates able to defile the saints of Yah. This is the on-going battle in which we will need His strength to stand against its fearsome attack. Stress is the number one 'dis-ease' of our country. This killer creates illnesses for which most individuals consume handfuls of prescription drugs daily. How can we prevent this stress from over taking the holy ones of Yah? Why are our souls not able to rest in Him? Why do we surrender victim to this disease of the new millennium?

Perhaps we do not fear Yah enough. Perhaps we are not thinking on the pure and lovely and all things worthy of praise. Perhaps we have let our eyes drift off of our goal, the mark of the high calling in Yahshua ha Machiach/Jesus the Messiah. Or perhaps we simply do not trust Him in His care of us; or His promises to us in His instruction manual. Are we letting the voices of the world, or non-believers over-ride the Voice of the Spirit? Who are we going to believe?

Let us learn to fear our Yah. Let us remember the awesome acts He did for our forefathers, Israel. Let us meditate on the miracles His is doing in our own lives today to keep us in the fear of our LORD.

Are you lacking anything in your life? Check your fear level. It may need adjusting.

Part Four

Heavenly Information

Dancing For You

DANCING FOR YOU

Dancing for You is what I want to do.
Let me experience You in every thing I do.
Let me dance on your gentle lips.
Spinning and twirling all around your sweet lips.
Let me flow through the words that you speak to create.
So I can be in all your creations.
Spin me around my Lord and watch me dance for You.
You are my King and my Lord.
Watch me dance for You.
I dance only for You.
I want to dance in You, through You and all around You.
Give this honor to me my King, so I can dance for You

C.C. Anderson
March 4th, 2001

All Israel Dances Toward The Tabernacle

QUICK REFERENCE GUIDE OF DANCE IN SCRIPTURE:

DANCE

1. JUDGES 21:21
2. JOB 21:11
3. PSALM 149:3, 150:4
4. ECCLESIASTES 3:4
5. ISAIAH 13:21
6. JEREMIAH 31:13
7. LAMENTATIONS 5:15

DANCED

1. JUDGES 21:23
2. 2 SAMUEL 6:14
3. MATTHEW 11:17, 14:6
4. MARK 6:22
5. LUKE 7:32

DANCES

1. EXODUS 15:20
2. JUDGES 11:34, 21:21
3. 1 SAMUEL 21:11, 29:5
4. JEREMIAH 31:4

DANCING

1. EXODUS 32:19
2. 1 SAMUEL 18:6, 30:16
3. 2 SAMUEL 6:16
4. 1 CHRONICLES 15:29
5. PSALMS 30:11
6. LUKE 15:25

DANCE
As It Appears in Scripture
(From the NIV)

DANCE

"When the girls of Shiloh come out to join in the dancing, then rush from the vineyards and each of you seize a wife from the girls of Shiloh and go to the land of Benjamin" (Judges 21:21).

"They send forth their children as a flock; their little ones dance about" (Job 21:11).

"Let them praise his name with dancing and make music to him with tambourine and harp" (Psalms 149:3).

"Praise him with tambourine and dancing, praise him with the strings and flute" (Psalms 150:4).

There is "a time to weep and a time to laugh, a time to mourn and a time to dance" (Ecclesiastes 3:4).

"But desert creatures will lie there, jackals will fill her houses; there the owls will dwell, and there the wild goats will leap about" (Isaiah 13:21).

"Then maidens will dance and be glad, young men and old as well. I will turn their mourning into gladness; I will give them comfort and joy instead of sorrow" (Jeremiah 31:13).

"Joy is gone from our hearts; our dancing has turned to mourning" (Lamentations 5:15).

DANCED

"So that is what the Benjamites did. While the girls were dancing, each man caught one and carried her off to be his wife. Then they returned to their inheritance and rebuilt the towns and settled in them" (Judges 21:23).

"David, wearing a linen ephod, danced before the LORD with all his might" (2 Samuel 6:14).

"We played the flute for you, and you did not dance; we sang a dirge, and you did not mourn" (Matthew 11:17).

"On Herod's birthday the daughter of Herodias danced for them and pleased Herod so much" (Matthew 14:6).

"When the daughter of Herodias came in and danced, she pleased Herod and his dinner guests. The king said to the girl, 'Ask me for anything you want, and I'll give it to you'" (Mark 6:22).

"They are like children sitting in the marketplace and calling out to each other: 'We played the flute for you, and you did not dance; we sang a dirge, and you did not cry'" (Luke 7:32).

DANCES

"Then Miriam the prophetess, Aaron's sister, took a tambourine in her hand, and all the women followed her, with tambourines and dancing" (Exodus 15:20).

"When Jephthah returned to his home in Mizpah, who should come out to meet him but his daughter, dancing to the sound of tambourines! She was an only child. Except for her he had neither son nor daughter" (Judges 11:34).

"When the girls of Shiloh come out to join in the dancing, then rush from the vineyards and each of you seize a wife from the girls of Shiloh and go to the land of Benjamin" (Judges 21:21).

"But the servants of Achish said to him, 'Isn't this David, the king of the land? Isn't he the one they sing about in their dances: "Saul has slain his thousands, and David his tens of thousands"?'" (1 Samuel 21:11).

"Isn't this the David they sang about in their dances: 'Saul has slain his thousands, and David his tens of thousands'?" (1 Samuel 29:5).

"I will build you up again and you will be rebuilt, O Virgin Israel. Again you will take up your tambourines and go out to dance with the joyful" (Jeremiah 31:4).

DANCING

"When Moses approached the camp and saw the calf and the dancing, his anger burned and he threw the tablets out of his hands, breaking them to pieces at the foot of the mountain" (Exodus 32:19).

"When the men were returning home after David had killed the Philistine, the women came out from all the towns of Israel to meet King Saul with singing and dancing, with joyful songs and with tambourines and lutes" (1 Samuel 18:6).

"He led David down, and there they were, scattered over the countryside, eating, drinking and reveling because of the great amount of plunder they had taken from the land of the Philistines and from Judah" (1 Samuel 30:16).

"As the ark of the LORD was entering the City of David, Michal daughter of Saul watched from a window. And when she saw King

David leaping and dancing before the LORD, she despised him in her heart" (2 Samuel 6:16).

"As the ark of the covenant of the LORD was entering the City of David, Michal daughter of Saul watched from a window. And when she saw King David dancing and celebrating, she despised him in her heart" (1 Chronicles 15:29).

"You turned my wailing into dancing; you removed my sackcloth and clothed me with joy" (Psalms 30:11).

"Meanwhile, the older son was in the field. When he came near the house, he heard music and dancing" (Luke 15:25).

All Israel Dances Toward The Tabernacle

Other Simchat Adonai Dance Materials To Come...

Interchangeable Dances for the 21st Century...

A workbook for those who love interchangeable dances. These circle dances are all brand new choreography.

How to Start Your Own Dance Ministry:

A workbook that trains dancers to be leaders in the dance in their own congregation or ministry.

Gathering Israel: A Musical on Video

Calling forth into unity every tribe and nation. Features Simchat Adonai Director Chester Anderson with special guests Dancers of Judah (led by DaVonne Miller). This video depicts the Two Houses of Israel. Through dance and drama Simchat Adonai shows how Israel was one people, was divided, and through the hand of the Father, become one people again.

New Messianic Israel Two House Art Work:

Coming 1/01/02. New and exciting art form, available January 2002. Some of the art can be seen in this book and will be available in larger sizes.

For more information contact:

Chester Anderson
simchatadonai@cfl.rr.com
or call:
352.307.3537

All Israel Dances Toward The Tabernacle

Abbreviations And Bibliography

Abbreviations:
CJB: *Complete Jewish Bible*
KJV: *King James Version* Bible
NASB: *New American Standard Bible*
NIV: *New International Version* Bible
STET: *The Stone Edition Tanach*
Strong's: *Strong's Concordance*

The following is a listing of writings used in making this book.

Green, Jay P. *The Interlinear Bible*, Hebrew, Greek, English. Grand Rapids: Baker, 1979.
New International Version Study Bible. Grand Rapids: Zondervan, 1995.
Strong, James. *The New Strong's Exhaustive Concordance*. Nashville: Thomas Nelson, 1984.
Stern, David H. *Jewish New Testament Commentary*. Clarksville, MD: Jewish New Testament, 1995.
_____*The Stone Edition Tanach*, Mesorah Publications, Brooklyn, NY., 1996-1998.
Webster's Third New International Dictionary, 3 Vols. Chicago: Encyclopedia Britannica, 1981.
Wootten, Angus. *Restoring Israel's Kingdom.* Saint Cloud, FL: Key of David, 2000.
Wootten, Batya Ruth. *Who Is Israel?* Saint Cloud, FL: Key of David, 2000.

All Israel Dances Toward The Tabernacle

Ten Tips To Help You Understand Israel

by Batya Wootten

1) Like the United States, Israel was once divided into Northern and Southern Kingdoms—and they have never been fully reunited (Jeremiah 3:14-18; Isaiah 11: 14; Zechariah 8:3-13; 10:7-10; Ezekiel 37:15-28).

2) Scripture calls these two kingdoms, "both the houses of Israel," Yahweh's "two nations," and, "the two families that Yahweh chose" (Isaiah 8:14; Ezekiel 35:10; 37:22; Jeremiah 33:23-26).

3) Those of Ephraim, the Northern Kingdom of Israel, were scattered among every nation, for they were destined to become a "melo hagoyim," a "fullness of Gentiles" (Hosea 1-2; 8:8; Amos 9:9; Romans 11).

4) The gifts and calling of the God of Israel are without repentance. Thus, on all Israel, both Judah and Ephraim, there remains an eternal call to love, and to be obedient to, the God of Israel (Deuteronomy 28:1-6; Numbers 23: 19; Isaiah 43:10; Romans 11:29).

5) The Ephraimites became degenerate, wild, olive branches. However, once returned to Israel's Olive Tree, they are called to provoke those of Judah to jealousy, to walk in a way that makes Judah want what they have (Jeremiah 11: 10,16; 2:18,21; Romans 11; 9:26; Hosea 1 :9,1; Isaiah 35:10).

6) As heirs of Abraham's promise, non-Jewish Believers in Messiah are brought nigh to, and share citizenship in, the commonwealth of Israel (Genesis 17:4-7; Romans 4:17; Galatians 3:29; Ephesians 2:11-22).

7) When the Father makes the "two sticks" of Ezekiel "one stick in His hand," thereafter, Israel is no more "plucked up" from the Land, they have "one king" (the King of Kings and Lord of Lords), and, they no longer defile themselves with "any" of their transgressions (Ezekie1 37: 15-28). Thus, a fully reunited Israel is a "sinless" Israel, one that lives under Messiah's rule, in the Land of Promise.

8) It is a perpetual statute that, after a "foreigner" called by the Father has fulfilled the three proscribed rules of circumcision, Passover, and sojourning, he thereafter must be regarded as a "native of the Land" (Exodus 12:48; Leviticus 19:34; Numbers 9: 14; Isaiah 56:3; Ephesians 2:11-19).

9) Jews and Christians—Judah and Ephraim—serve as "two witnesses" for the God of Israel, and they now need to serve their divine purpose, which is to "confirm" His truth in the Earth (Numbers 35:30; Deuteronomy 17:6; 19:15; John 8:17; 2 Corinthians 13:1).

10) Israel was to be a "mystery" until the "fullness of Gentiles," the "*melo hagoyim*" promised to Ephraim "be come in." So it is that, in this last, day the veil is being lifted, and we are now coming to understand the truth about all Israel, both houses (Romans 11:25; Genesis 48:19; Jeremiah 31:18,19).

Reprinted from the book *Who Is Israel? A Study Guide*, companion to the book, *Who Is Israel?* by Batya Wootten
Available through:
Key of David, PO Box 700217, Saint Cloud, FL, 34770
1.800.829.8777   Web: www.mim.net
Used by Permission.

Simchat Adonai Dance Ministry

The dance ministry of Simchat Adonai (Joy of the Lord), which was established in 1997 by Chester Anderson, has been given a diverse ministry from the heart of Abba, our Heavenly Father. Our first priority continues to be the ministry to Abba in praise and worship at the foot of His throne (this is our vertical ministry). As we minister in the "art" of dance in conferences, workshops and congregational settings, we minister to the 'body of Messiah,' bringing them into the presence of our King (this is our horizontal ministry). As dance ministers, we teach, not only the basic dance steps but also instruct all who have an ear to hear what the Ruach/Spirit is saying to the His congregations concerning worship, and specifically, dance.

We encourage everyone to dance before the Father. Through dance, all people will be united as one. This is one of our main goals in Simchat Adonai. Bringing Jews and Christians into the knowledge of unity through dance as worship.

Simchat Adonai dance ministry is available to come to serve your congregation in any and all aspects of dance. We instruct from the Word of Yahweh, our God, to lay a strong and deep foundation for dance. We can come to minister in dance at your times of worship and/or we can come to give instruction in dance by conducting a dance seminar. The Father has given us a multi versatile ministry in the arts, which includes Messianic, interpretive, tambourine, ballet, flags and contemporary 'Christian' dance. Dance seminars are fun for worshipers of all ages, male or female, whether one has had any prior dance experience. As we fulfill the command of Yahweh, our lives are blessed.

Praise the Lord. Sing to the Lord a new song, His praise is the assembly of the saints. Let Israel rejoice in their Maker; let the people of Zion be glad in their King. Let them praise his name with dancing and make music to Him with tambourine and harp.

For information and engagements concerning Simchat Adonai, contact:

Chester Anderson
simchatadonai@cfl.rr.com
352.307.3537

Or

Tina Clemens
joybubbles@cheerful.com

Notes

Notes